Costs and Benefits

of Education

COSTS AND BENEFITS

OF EDUCATION

ROBERT D. LEITER
Editor

90692

ANNUAL VOLUME OF THE DEPARTMENT OF ECONOMICS

CITY COLLEGE

of the

CITY UNIVERSITY OF NEW YORK

VOLUME I

TWAYNE PUBLISHERS

A DIVISION OF G. K. HALL & CO., BOSTON

Preface

The will of the late Harry Schwager, a distinguished alumnus of the City College of New York, class of June 1911, left to the Economics Department a sum of money whose income is to be employed for economic projects. The members of the Department agreed that the best use of the bequest would be to sponsor an annual conference on an importment topical issue and subsequently publish the papers delivered in a regular series of volumes.

The first conference on "Costs and Benefits of Education" was held on May 17, 1973. Eight papers were presented, six of which were followed by discussion. One of the papers, delivered by the Honorable Murry Bergtraum, a member of the Board of Education of the City of New York, dealing with cost effectiveness of public expenditures for education, is unfortunately not available for publication. On the other hand, a paper sent in to the Department by Professor Walter I. Garms before the conference could not be delivered, but was included in the volume along with some comments.

Help in reading and criticizing the manuscripts submitted and in selecting those accepted was a time-consuming burden which many of my colleagues cheerfully shared. They include Professors James Arrowsmith, Richard D. Auster, Malcolm Galatin, William I. Greenwald, Benjamin J. Klebaner, Akundi Rao, Stephen Resnick, Edwin P. Reubens, Morris Silver, and Gerald Sirkin. Much of the credit for the success of the project is due to the constant concern, timely encouragement, and valuable suggestions of the Chairman of the Department, Professor Morris Silver.

5

It is the hope of the Department that the legacy of Harry Schwager will be used to develop and expand important areas of economic knowledge and public concern.

ROBERT D. LEITER

City College of the City University of New York

Contents

Some Background to Studies of the Costs and Benefits of Education

Robert D. Leiter*

The impact of formal education on the economic and social well-being of individuals and society in the United States has been under intense statistical study by scholars during the past fifteen years. But although the research has been late in coming, it is not unexpected. At least from the time of the founding fathers, this country has stressed its faith in education as a means of bringing about social change. Thomas Jefferson, Horace Mann, and John Dewey are illustrious names in this tradition.

Some of the important public policies and controversies in the field of education stem from the 1954 decision of the United States Supreme Court in *Brown* v. *School Board of Topeka,* where the Court held that segregation which is permitted by law is injurious to Negroes and that racially segregated schools are inherently unequal. Thus the long standing doctrine enunciated by the Court in 1896 in *Plessy* v. *Ferguson* that separate but equal facilities for blacks and whites does not conflict with the United States Constitution was overturned.

Subsequent to the decision of 1954, in which the Court reinforced public confidence in education as a means of improving the economic and social position of members of minorities, the federal government set out to equalize the educational opportunities available to all groups. Progress in breaking down segregation barriers in the schools was slow, but President Lyndon B. Johnson undertook especially vigorous action under the Civil Rights Act of 1964. Among other things, this law mandated a study of educational opportunity in the United States and led to the widely circulated

*Professor of Economics, City College of the City University of New York.

document appearing in 1966 known as the Coleman Report. The findings of James S. Coleman in *Equality of Educational Opportunity* shook the foundations of liberal thinking concerning education. He concluded that academic achievement of students is relatively independent of the quality of the schools they attend, if quality is measured by expenditures per pupil, teachers' salaries and degrees, pupil-teacher ratios, laboratory and library facilities, and similar yardsticks. Only when children study with classmates from affluent homes is there a consistent positive relationship to test performance. Furthermore, achievement is negligibly affected by desegregation. He found that a large part of the variation in student achievement lies within schools rather than between schools. The home and family background of children is the most important factor affecting achievement. Coleman did suggest, however, that spending in some specific areas, such as remedial reading, may lead to better test results.

The Coleman Report focused attention on the costs of education and the benefits of education. Each of these categories may be considered from the point of view of private and public investment decisions; that is, individuals and their families on the one hand (though it is important to realize that separate analyses of those two groups might be useful, as their interests and concerns do not necessarily coincide), and society on the other. Costs and benefits are measured mainly in monetary terms, but nonmonetary elements may also be considered. Private costs include tuition and forgone earnings during the period of formal education; public costs cover all the expenditures for schools. Private and public benefits are the income increase to the individuals or society resulting from the investments made. Public and private benefits may also diverge, however, because persons other than investors participate in the effects of such expenditures. These *external* effects include, among others, reduction in criminal and antisocial behavior, civic contributions, and concern for the environment.

The Coleman Report intensified the controversy as to whether spending more funds for schools in poor communities will improve educational attainments of students. Many persons have maintained intuitive faith in the notion that increased spending is the basis for

ɔnal level of pupils.
ɣ empirical studies have concluded that more
ɟ greater achievement, most studies have been less
of the more important issues of the past decade
extent, if any, of the genetic component of variation
in ,   e, the difference between true integration and simple
deseg.   ɔn, and the advent of diminishing returns in educational expenditures.

The most recent study attracting national attention was completed by Christopher Jencks with the assistance of Harvard University scholars. In 1972, he authored *Inequality: A Reassessment of the Effect of Family and Schooling in America*, a volume that went well beyond the conclusions reached by Coleman. Jencks found that more expensive schooling for poor children has little effect on their prospects for economic success as adults. He estimated that 75 per cent of the variation in income among persons is due to luck or to elusive and unmeasured differences in personality and ability to handle the job held, rather than schooling, intelligence quotients, or family background. Specifically, regarding education, neither racial desegregation, compensatory education, preschool programs, or additional school expenditures significantly affect inequality in cognitive skill; that is, ability to manipulate words and numbers, assimilate information, and make logical inferences. The characteristics of the children entering school are of prime importance in cognitive skill development. School budgets, school policies, and teacher characteristics are irrelevant or of secondary importance.

In his paper in this volume, Morris Silver cogently challenges the notion that better schools cannot be obtained by spending more money. He stresses that the current debate regarding the impact of school resources on student performance ignores the fact that school inputs are not an exogenous variable but are determined in part by student performance.

A specific contribution of economists to the evolving public concern with costs and benefits of education as they affect different groups in society has been the refinement of the human capital concept. This idea has led to studies that deal mainly with investment in human beings in the form of education. The studies attempt to determine the effect of such expenditures on future earnings and productivity of the individual and the economy, and to determine the rate of return.

Prior to the investment in human capital approach, economists had considered the main factors responsible for differential earnings among individuals to be differences in ability and opportunity. The ongoing research by Gary S. Becker and Jacob Mincer has linked earnings closely to the extent or length of formal schooling and subsequent training. Differences in earnings among individuals are related also to age and experience, after the period of formal education, involving mobility, leisure, attitudes, and health. It has shown that discounting future income returns made the postponement of earnings far more important in accounting for the differences resulting from increased education than did the shorter working life of those who go to school longer.

Reservations and new insights about the human capital model are expressed in several papers. Charles R. McKnew, Jr. and David G. Tuerck reject the argument that educational opportunity costs alone are useful for prescribing public fiscal policy toward education or for predicting student behavior. They contend that account must be taken of the satisfaction obtained from the schooling itself. Several additional gaps in the human capital approach are suggested in R. D. Auster's comments. M. O. Clement and Alan Gustman are concerned with the response of the student and his family to the quality of schools. They link the variations in enrollment among states for vocational education at the high school level to relative expenditures by the states on vocational educational programs, socioeconomic and ethnic background of the students, and availability of economic opportunities for those completing the programs.

The work of scholars dealing with investment in human capital differs from that of sociologists, psychologists, and educators comparing the schooling of different groups of children mainly in that the former stresses the relationship between more education and higher income rather than the effects of similar education under varying amounts of expenditures. Many unanswered questions remain regarding measurement of the changes in the quality of education as distinguished from variation in the sums of money spent. There is still much work to be done to determine which school inputs are closely associated with increased quality education.

Some papers in this volume deal with various aspects of costs and benefits of education that have hitherto been completely neglected. Walter I. Garms shows that the fifty states allocate funds differently between higher and lower education. He sets forth the determinants of expenditure per capita for each of the two categories and compares the predicted values based on the determinants with the actual values. Edmund H. Mantell studies some persons who are excluded from the engineering labor market because their formal education is inadequate. Yet these persons would have a higher marginal product in the engineering labor market than in the market where they are employed. He finds that education-based employment discrimination exists in the engineering labor market. George M. Vredeveld concludes that state subsidies for public education generally serve to create a flow of wealth from low income to high income classes. James V. Koch applies a linear programming model to the process of resource allocation at a university. The model is intended to help college administrators allocate efficiently scarce resources, such as money and space, to fit the specific decision criteria of the institution. Finally, Edwin P. Reubens discusses whether the costs and benefits of international migrations of skilled persons may always be analyzed as being at the expense of the country from which emigration occurs and to the benefit of those that receive immigrants. All but one of the papers in this volume are followed by critical comments.

1

The Prediction of State-Local Expenditures for Higher and Lower Education in the United States

Walter I. Garms*

This paper reports on a portion of a larger study concerned with the effort made by state and local governments to support education in the United States. It particularly focuses on the dichotomy of higher education and lower education[1] and the fact that various states are very different in the relative emphasis they put on support of higher education as compared with their support of lower education. This paper examines separately the determinants of state-local governmental expenditure per capita for higher education (HE/Cap), and for Lower education (LE/Cap), using the state as the unit of analysis. It then compares the ratio of the predicted values of HE/Cap to LE/Cap (equivalent to the ratio of total state-local expenditures for higher education to those for lower education, designated HE/LE) with the actual values of HE/LE. It also compares the efficiency of predicting the ratio in this manner with that of making a single prediction of HE/LE, as was done in another part of the study.

There have been a number of investigations of the determinants of expenditures for lower education. The various previous investigations have tested determinants that can usually be classified into three general categories: ability to support education, demand for education, and political or governmental variables. The ability and

*University of Rochester. This paper is based on research done under a Ford Foundation grant during 1971–72.

demand variables have proven to be generally good predictors of expenditures; the political and governmental variables have been less successful. The rationale developed here borrows heavily from other investigations, but attempts, in the governmental area, to find variables not previously used, and which are subject to change by state policy-makers. The rationales explaining HE/Cap and LE/Cap are similar. We shall first consider lower education.

Clearly, the best measure of ability to support educational expenditures is some measure of income. The measure chosen here is personal income per capita.

Demand for education can be separated conceptually into a quantitative demand, representing the physical number of students to be educated, and a qualitative demand, representing the desire of the adult population of a state for more and better education for each student. The quantitative demand will be measured by two variables. One is the relative proportion of school-age children in the population. The exact measure is the number of children aged five to seventeen as a percentage of the total population (5–17/Pop). The other would be a measure of the propensity to invest in private education instead of public education. It is tempting simply to measure the percentage of students enrolled in private schools in each state. But to measure the effect begs the question of why there are such differences among the states. It would seem much better to find a variable with more explanatory interest.

For lower education, such a variable is relatively easy to find. Nationally, in 1965-66, 88% of elementary and 81% of secondary non-public school enrollment was Roman Catholic. Thus it appears that a measure of Roman Catholics as a percentage of the population would be a good variable to explain the extent to which elementary and secondary students are siphoned off to non-public schools. The measure will be referred to as Catholics/Pop. The greater is the percentage of Catholics in the population, the less support one might expect for governmental expenditures on lower education.

The qualitative demand is measured by the percentage of the adult population who have had at least some college (Ed Level), on the assumption that better-educated adults will demand better quality education for their children. (Median years of schooling of the adult population has frequently been used as a variable measuring this factor. Percent with some higher education is highly correlated with median years schooling, and is used because it can also be used as a variable in explaining higher education expenditures, where it appears to have a conceptual advantage. The greatest difficulty with either schooling variable is that it is only measured decennially, with the most recent data available at the time of the study being for 1960.)

Previous studies have been generally unsuccessful in finding any measures of governmental arrangements that were significant. However, this investigator has argued elsewhere that access to decision-making by the public is sufficiently similar in various parts of the United States that measures of political structure (such as fiscal dependence or independence of school districts) are not significant.[2] On the other hand, there are some measures of government that are of potential importance that have not been well tested previously. One is a measure of the extractive capability of a government. This is a measure of the ability of a government, through taxes and other means, to extract money for public purposes from its citizens. It is measured here as total dollars of state and local general revenue raised for all purposes per $1,000 of personal income.

A second governmental measure is the relative extractive capability of state governments compared with local governments. This is the ratio of state-raised revenue to locally-raised revenue. State money constitutes about 90% of the state-local funds to higher education, whereas nationally more than half of the money for lower education comes from local taxes. Thus it might be expected that a state like South Carolina, where the ratio of state-raised revenue to locally-raised revenue was about 2.4 in 1967, would do a relatively better job, other things being equal, of providing money for higher education (and a poorer job of providing money for lower education) than a state such as New Jersey, where the ratio was only 0.6. The variable is referred to as Tax Ratio.

The third governmental variable used here is a measure of the elasticity of state taxes. The reasoning is that in a period of rapidly increasing demand for governmental expenditures, the state which has the more elastic tax structure may be best able to satisfy the demands. The difficulty with this measure conceptually is that it is difficult to state what will happen to education when not all demands upon the government can be met. Will education get the short end of the stick, or will it fare better proportionately? It seems worthwhile to try it and see. From a practical standpoint, the variable has two problems. First, we have been able only to locate data for 1968. This makes longitudinal comparisons impossible. Second, the data found are only a measure of the elasticity of certain state taxes (individual income taxes, general sales, and selected sales taxes). Other state taxes, and the local property tax, are excluded. Nevertheless, this is the best measure available, and it appears worth trying as a variable.

Turning to state-local governmental expenditures for higher education, it appears that similar variables could be used to predict. Ability could be measured by personal income per capita, as with lower education. The first element of the quantitative demand for higher education, number of individuals eligible, could be measured by the proportion of the population aged 18 through 20 (18–20/Pop).

The second element of quantitative demand, having to do with propensity to send students to private higher education, deserves more discussion. A religious variable does not serve as well to describe private higher education attendance. Nationally, private higher education enrollment in 1967 (classified according to the religious denomination with which colleges considered themselves affiliated) was 53% independent, 23% Protestant, 21% Catholic, and 2% other (mostly Mormon). It appears more fruitful to look to history for a variable. Private institutions of higher education were established in this country long before public institutions. These private institutions were established in areas where a sufficient concentration of population existed to create a demand for higher education. Beginning with the Morrill Act (which established the land-grant colleges) immediately after the Civil War, substantial public money was poured into colleges. The private colleges that had already been established persisted, but particularly in states where there had been no previous tradition of private colleges, few new ones were founded. If this analysis is true, a measure of population density of the states in a year immediately previous to the Morrill Act would be a good variable to explain the percentage of students attending private institutions today. The measure that has been chosen is the number of persons per square mile in each state in 1860, and the variable will be referred to as 1860 Density. It is hypothesized that the greater was population density in 1860, the greater is present support for private higher education, and the less is support for public higher education.

As with lower education, the percentage of adults who had some college training (Ed Level) is used as a measure of the relative demand for quality as well as quantity of higher education.

Here also, the governmental factors that seem worth investigating are extractive capability (Extract), relative extractive capability (Tax Ratio), and elasticity of the tax structure (Elasticity).

Because personal income per capita appears *prima facie* to be such an important variable, some preliminary investigation of its effect by itself was made. State and local governmental expenditures per capita for lower education tend to rise with increased personal income per capita. The correlation between the two is about .72, indicating that personal income per capita explains about 52% of the variation in state and local governmental expenditures per capita for lower education. On the other hand, there is little or no correlation between state and local governmental expenditures for higher education and personal income per capita. The correlation between them of .08 indicates that less than 1% of the variation in HE/Cap is accounted for by personal income per capita, and such a small correlation is almost certainly the result of random variation in the values of the variables. This difference between lower and higher education would appear to be a significant finding which deserves more investigation.

A possible explanation might be that elementary and secondary school teachers tend to look for jobs in a statewide market, but not to any great extent in a national market. Statewide credentialling requirements with little interstate reciprocity would be one reason for this. On the other hand, it appears probable that higher education faculty deal in a nationwide market. This would mean that salaries for elementary and secondary teachers could fluctuate with personal income per capita among the states, but that higher education faculty salaries would be much more even across the country (or would, at least, vary in ways that had little to do with personal income per capita in the state). Then, since faculty salaries constitute the major portion of current expenditures, one would expect current expenditures per student to be highly correlated with personal income per capita in lower education, but not in higher education. Current expenditures per student in lower education are indeed highly correlated with personal income per capita ($r = .95$), whereas higher education instructional expenditures per degree-credit student are much more scattered, with a correlation of less than .05. Thus, this brief analysis tends to support the hypothesis.

The implication is that in a multiple regression predicting LE/Cap, personal income should be an important predictor, but in a regression predicting HE/Cap, it should be relatively unimportant.

Multiple regressions were done for 1961–62 and 1967–68, predicting LE/Cap and HE/Cap. The 1967–68 data were the most recent available; the 1961–62 data represent the end of a long period of apparent relative stability extending from the early 1950s. The results are shown in Table 1.

It is clear that the variables used do a better job of predicting expenditures per capita for lower education than for higher education, which is to be expected because of the diversity of higher education and the fact that attendance is not universal. It is interesting to note that for lower education the predictive value of the variables is just as good in 1967–68 as in 1961–62, but for higher education the predictive ability of the variables has declined substantially from 1961–62 to 1967–68.

Looking at the standard regression coefficients, it can be observed that Personal Income is by far the best predictor of LE/Cap in both years. It is not such a good predictor of HE/Cap in either year, although it is a substantially better predictor in 1967–68 than in 1961–62. The findings are consistent with what had been expected by examining the relationship of Personal Income and

TABLE 1
PREDICTION OF STATE-LOCAL GOVERNMENTAL EXPENDITURES PER CAPITA
FOR EDUCATION

Expenditures for Lower Education	1961-62	1967-68
Coefficient of determination (R^2)	.84	.84
Standard regression coefficients (beta weights)		
Personal Income	.95**	.78**
5-17/Pop	.40**	.18
Catholics/Pop	−.04	.01
Ed Level	.28*	.11
Extract	.23	.31**
Tax Ratio	−.05	−.12
Elasticity	—	.08
Expenditures for Higher Education		
Coefficient of determination (R^2)	.75	.68
Standard regression coefficients (beta weights)		
Personal Income	.23	.42**
18-20/Pop	−.09	.09
1860 Density	−.43**	−.38**
Ed Level	.27	−.04
Extract	.46**	.61**
Tax Ratio	.08	−.16
Elasticity	—	−.04

*Significant at .05 level.
**Significant at .01 level.

either LE/Cap or HE/Cap without controlling for other variables. An alternative hypothesis that people with higher incomes are more apt to send their children to private higher education is not refuted by this finding. But to the extent it is true (which would postulate a negative relationship between Personal Income and HE/Cap), it is overbalanced by the tendency of people with higher income to spend more on public higher education too. This is so because the regression coefficient of Personal Income in predicting HE/Cap is positive, although not as large as it is in predicting LE/Cap.

The best predictor of HE/Cap in both years is Extract. It is the second best predictor of LE/Cap in 1967–68, and the fourth best predictor in 1961–62. Clearly, it is an important variable, and one that has been too little used in other investigations.

The two measures of propensity to invest in private education show differing tendencies. Catholics/Pop, as a measure of propensity to invest in private lower education, is not a significant variable in either year. But 1860 Denisty, as a measure of propensity to invest in private higher education, is the second best predictor in 1961–62, and the third best in 1967–68.

The measure of the relative number of students to be educated (5–17/Pop for LE/Cap and 18–20/Pop for HE/Cap) is a good predictor for LE/Cap in 1961–62, but is disappointing in 1967–68, and is disappointing for HE/Cap in both years. This may result from use of a variable which has relatively little variability. The measure of demand represented by the education of adults in the population (Ed Level) is also rather disappointing, particularly in 1967–68. The poor performance in 1967–68 may result from being forced to use 1960 Ed Level data instead of 1970 data.

Finally, Tax Ratio and Elasticity show themselves to have no significant predictive ability.

To test whether any predictive ability was lost by using the conceptually more satisfying variables of Catholics/Pop instead of private lower ed students as a percent of total lower ed students (Pvt. LE Stud/Total), and 1860 Density instead of private higher ed students as a percent of total higher ed students (Pvt. HE Stud/Total), regressions were done substituting these variables, with the following results for R^2:

	1961 - 62	1967 - 68
Lower Education		
Using Catholics/Pop (and other variables as in Table 1)	.84	.84
Using Pvt. LE Stud/Total	.85	.84

Higher Education

Using 1860 Density	.75	.68
Using Pvt. HE Stud/Total	.74	.65

It is apparent that the conceptually more satisfying variables are also at least as good as predictors, and may be a little better. And it is certainly an interesting commentary on the persistence of historical trends that one of the best predictors of governmental expenditures on higher education in the 1960s was the density of population 100 years earlier.

The final step in the analysis is to take the ratio of the predicted values for HE/Cap and LE/Cap and compare them with the actual values for HE/LE. The results are as follows:

	1961 - 62	1967 - 68
Using 18-20/5-17, Ed Level, Catholics/Pop 1860 Density, Tax Ratio, Personal Income and Extract to predict HE/LE directly	.67	.53
Using the variables discussed in this chapter to predict HE/Cap and LE/Cap separately, then correlating the ratio of the predicted values of HE/Cap and LE/Cap with actual values of HE/LE	.57	.46

It is clear that if one is interested in the relative public provision for higher and lower education, one can do a better job of predicting the ratio directly than by predicting its components separately. However, the apparent greater efficiency may simply be the result of allowing the multiple regression technique to take all of the random variation of the variables directly into account. If so, the differences between the R^2 values obtained in predicting the ratio and those of the ratio of the predictions are merely statistical artifacts. The choice of which method of analysis to use then becomes one of which gives the better conceptual insights. The two methods give somewhat different insights, and it is probably valuable to use both, particularly since one can derive the data for one from the data for the other. But the analysis of HE/Cap and LE/Cap separately has given some insights into the variations in the ratio that could not have been obtained directly.

Assuming that investigation of the determinants of HE/Cap and LE/Cap for other years shows substantially the same pattern as is shown for these two years, a new rationale might shape up something as follows:

1. Lower education has been overwhelmingly accepted in the U.S. as a responsibility of the state, rather than an individual responsibility. It is the largest single responsibility of state and local governments. As a result, the amount of public money spent per capita on lower education (LE/Cap) is primarily determined by the amount of money available, and this is a function of the personal income per capita and the percentage of that personal income that can be extracted from the populace by state and local governments. LE/Cap as determined by these ability variables (one representing personal ability, the other governmental ability), is modified somewhat by the influence of the number at an appropriate age to be educated, and by the demand of the more highly educated parents for better education for their children. Because of the overwhelming majority of the population who are in favor of public lower education, religiously induced propensity to support private education is not a strong influence on LE/Cap.

2. Higher education has been much more heterogeneous than lower education. Private higher education enrollment has only become less than 50% of the total in the decade of the sixties. Income has come from a variety of sources, even in the public institutions. Attendance at higher education institutions by those at the appropriate age level is nowhere near universal, as it is with lower education. Thus, higher education has not the compelling pull on the public purse that lower education has, and the ability of the population to support higher education is not as important as it is with lower education. On the other hand, the ability of the government, as measured by its extractive capability, is even more important. It may be that higher education, as a less mandatory responsibility of government, has a higher elasticity of demand upon the state's re-

sources. The fact that attendance is not universal makes the relative percentage of the population at the appropriate age level unimportant, but a tradition-based propensity to invest in private higher education is a most important determinant.

Because we are also interested in the ratio of higher education to lower education expenditures, there are some advantages to using the same variables to explain both HE/Cap and LE/Cap, since these could then also be used to predict HE/LE. (There is some discussion of a better model for this at the end of this paper.) The use of identical variables presents no great problem, since the variables are already substantially the same. The differences are in the variables measuring propensity to invest in private education and in proportion of the population at the appropriate age for the level of education being considered. The present formulation thinks of Catholics/Pop as a measure of propensity to invest in private lower education, and 1860 Density as a measure of propensity to invest in private higher education. One could instead think of Catholics/Pop as a measure of religiously-induced propensity to invest in private education (higher and lower), and of 1860 Density as a measure of tradition-induced propensity to invest in private education (higher and lower). The use of both variables in predicting both HE/Cap and LE/Cap would be legitimate, and possibly significantly increase the explanation of variance.

It is more difficult to defend the use of 18–20/Pop as a variable in explaining LE/Cap, or 5–17/Pop as a variable in explaining HE/Cap. But it is not at all certain that these are variables of real practical value for use as determinants (because of their limited variation among states), although they have theoretical significance. Thus, these variables have been omitted in the regressions below.

This revised rationale was then tested on data for a number of additional years for which data were available. Regressions predicting HE/Cap and LE/Cap were done for these years using as independent variables Personal Income, Extract, 1860 Density, Catholics/Pop, and Ed Level. The results are presented in Table 2. It is apparent that using these variables it is possible to predict about 80% of the variation in LE/Cap and 70% of the variation in HE/Cap. While the ability to predict variation in HE/Cap has de-

TABLE 2

PREDICTION OF HE/CAP AND LE/CAP FOR SEVEN BIENNIA

Predicting LE/Cap	1953-54	1957-58	1959-60	1961-62	1963-64	1965-66	1967-68
R^2	.81	.74	.84	.84	.76	.84	.83
Beta Weights							
Personal Income	.74**	.83**	.77**	.77**	.70**	.87**	.78**
Extract	.25*	.30*	.37**	.24*	.23	.44**	.33**
1860 Density	-.19	-.21	-.31**	-.19	-.11	.00	-.11
Catholics/Pop	-.23	-.21	-.06	-.12	-.06	-.22	.02
Ed Level	.36**	.24	.27**	.29**	.27*	.13	.16
Predicting HE/Cap							
R^2	.69	.66	.76	.75	.76	.72	.68
Beta weights							
Personal Income	.40**	.31	.36**	.33*	.36**	.39**	.39**
Extract	.73**	.38*	.57**	.53**	.50**	.59**	.49**
1860 Density	-.40**	-.50**	-.40**	-.38**	-.33*	-.37**	-.49**
Catholics/Pop	-.14	.01	-.11	-.10	-.17	-.09	.18
Ed Level	.21	.22	.19	.21	.21	.02	-.01

*Significant at .05 level

**Significant at .01 level

clined from 75% to 68% between 1963–64 and 1967–68, the ability of the variables to predict variation in LE/Cap increased during the same period. The ability to predict both variables was better in 1967–68 than it was in 1957–58 in spite of the fact that it has been necessary to use 1960 data on Ed Level in 1967–68. Over the period of 14 years covered by these data, the ability of these variables to predict a very substantial percentage of variation in HE/Cap and LE/Cap has continued.

Table 2 shows the beta weights for the variables in these regressions. Comparison with Table 1 shows that these five variables do as good an overall job of prediction as the seven variables used there.

The patterns of the beta weights bring some insights. In spite of a very low correlation of Personal Income with HE/Cap (for example, in 1961-62 it is only .08), when 1860 Density and Extract are taken into account, personal income becomes an important predictor. Extract is the most important predictor, with Personal Income and 1860 Density being second and third, and of about equal importance. Catholics/Pop exerts a minor influence on HE/Cap, and usually a negative one. Ed Level has been of moderate importance, but its importance has declined in the most recent years (perhaps because of obsolete data).

For LE/Cap, Personal Income is by far the most important predictor. Extract is also important, but is not as important as it is in predicting HE/Cap. Ed Level is of more importance in explaining LE/Cap than HE/Cap, although here, too, its importance has declined in the most recent years. 1860 Density has been of minor importance in predicting LE/Cap, and its importance has declined in recent years. Catholics/Pop has ranged from being of minor importance to being of little or no importance in predicting LE/Cap.

To test the extent to which the regression coefficients could be considered as being essentially the same during the years covered, the regression coefficients for 1961–62 were used on the data for all of the other years, and the correlation of predicted values with actual values for HE/Cap and LE/Cap compared with the R^2 values obtained in the multiple regressions. The results were as follows:

	Predicting HE/Cap		Predicting LE/Cap	
Year	R² using 1961-62 coefficients	R² using own coefficients	R² using 1961-62 coefficients	R² using own coefficients
1953-54	.67	.69	.80	.81
1957-58	.65	.66	.73	.74
1959-60	.76	.76	.81	.84
1963-64	.76	.76	.75	.76
1965-66	.70	.72	.81	.84
1967-68	.59	.68	.78	.83

It is clear that, with the exception of 1967–68, the regression coefficients for 1961–62 do almost as good a job as the regression coefficients for each year developed by a multiple regression on the data for that year. We can thus have a good deal of confidence that the regression coefficients (and by implication, the effect of the variables) has remained stable over time. Whether 1967–68 is a unique exception, or whether there is a substantial change in the relationships beginning at the time is impossible to answer until time passes and more data become available.

These results tend to reinforce the speculations made a few pages earlier about the influences operating to determine LE/Cap and HE/Cap in the U.S. It is clear that those states with a substantial tradition of private higher educaiton have been able to meet the aspirations of their citizens for higher education with a lower outlay per capita of public money. It would appear to be to the financial advantage of those states to insure the continued financial health of their private institutions of higher education through whatever means seem appropriate. On the other hand, the heavy dependence of HE/Cap on the extractive capability of the state indicates the difficulty of giving more assistance to higher education without increasing appropriations for all other public purposes also. Those states presently with low extractive capabilities could consider this alternative; the states presently with high extractive capabilities may have to look more to the federal government. In any case, it is interesting that the percentage of adults who have attended college (Ed Level) has little independent effect on HE/Cap. It appears that our faith in higher education has transcended educational differences, with people of all educational backgrounds willing to support it as an avenue for economic success and social mobility for their children. Finally, as had been originally hypothesized, the percentage of Catholics in the population affects HE/Cap very little. Catholic higher education has never been as important a part of the American scene as Catholic lower education, and it is becoming less so.

Turning to lower education, the extremely heavy dependence of LE/Cap on personal income per capita helps to indicate the extent to which we would have a problem in trying to achieve equality of educational opportunity among the states. The differences in lower education expenditures per capita among the states are primarily due to differences in financial ability, and these differences can only be lessened through the auspices of the federal government. Extractive capability of the state is certainly of some importance, and as with higher education, those states with low extractive capabilities can think of raising them. Tradition-based propensity to invest in private lower education (measured by 1860 Density) has been minor and growing less important as a determinant of LE/Cap, and the same is true of a religion-induced propensity to invest in lower education. It appears that lower education is becoming ever more massively public.

A better formulation to test the above rationale would be the double log transformation. The form of the regression formula used above is

$$Y = a_0 + a_1 X_1 + a_2 X_2 + a_3 X_3 \ldots + a_n X_n,$$

where Y is the dependent variable, the X's are the values of the independent variables, and the a's are regression coefficients. If one takes the logarithm of all variables, a new regression is obtained:

$$\log Y = b_0 + b_1 \log X_1 + b_2 \log X_2 + b_3 \log X_3 \ldots + b_n \log X_n.$$

This equation can equivalently be written

$$Y = B \cdot X_1{}^{b1} \cdot X_2{}^{b2} \cdot X_3{}^{b3} \cdot \ldots \cdot X_n{}^{bn},$$

where $\log B = b_0$. In this formulation, the b values are partial elasticities of Y with respect to the X variables. That is, *ceteris paribus*, a 1% change in X_i will cause a $b_i\%$ change in Y. The advantage of this form of the equation becomes obvious when one combines the equations for HE/Cap and LE/Cap to get the equation for HE/LE. Let the two be as follows:

$$HE/Cap = B \cdot X_1{}^{b1} \cdot X_2{}^{b2} \cdot X_3{}^{b3} \cdot \ldots \cdot X_n{}^{bn}, \text{ and}$$

$$LE/Cap = C \cdot X_1{}^{c1} \cdot X_2{}^{c2} \cdot X_3{}^{c3} \cdot \ldots \cdot X_n{}^{cn}.$$

$$\text{Then } HE/LE = \frac{B}{C} \cdot X_1{}^{b1-c1} \cdot X_2{}^{b2-c2} \cdot X_3{}^{b3-c3} \cdot \ldots \cdot X_n{}^{bn-cn}$$

Put in log form, the three equations are

$$\log HE/Cap = b_0 + b_1 \log X_1 + b_2 \log X_2 + b_3 \log X_3 + \ldots + b_n \log X_n$$

$$\log LE/Cap = c_0 + c_1 \log X_1 + c_2 \log X_2 + c_3 \log X_3 + \ldots + c_n \log X_n$$

$$\log HE/LE = k + (b_1 - c_1) \log X_1 + (b_2 - c_2) \log X_2 + (b_3 - c_3) \log X_3 + \ldots + (b_n - c_n) \log X_n,$$

where $b_0 = \log B$, $c_0 = \log C$, and $k = \log B - \log C$.

It is seen from this that the partial elasticities of the ratio HE/LE with respect to the independent variables are simply the differences of the partial elasticities of the separate dependent variables with respect to these independent variables. The concept of the determinants of the ratio being dependent upon the determinants of the numerator and denominator is here built into the mathematical formulation. This could well be a fruitful approach, and the author intends to pursue this in the future, as well as investigating with more recent data the question of whether the determinants of HE/Cap and LE/Cap changed substantially on a more or less permanent basis in 1967–68.

NOTES

1. The term "lower education" is used for convenience to designate all formal education through twelfth grade. "Elementary-secondary education" is perhaps the more frequently used term, but "lower education" is shorter and emphasizes the dichotomy with higher education which is the concern of the study. Higher education refers to all formal education after grade twelve.

2. Walter I. Garms, *Multiple Correlates of Educational Expenditures by Nations*. Unpublished Ph.D. dissertation, Stanford University, 1967.

Comments on "The Prediction of State-Local Expenditures for Higher and Lower Education in the United States"
Akundi S. Rao*

This is a highly interesting study of the factors influencing the expenditures made by the governments, state and local, for higher and lower education. I feel that this study should be regarded more as an attempt to find the determinants of higher and lower education expenditures than as a model for prediction purposes or providing direct policy implications. The author, of course, does not claim that the investigation reported here has policy implications, but the only significant variable that the author speaks of as being "subject to change by the state policy-makers" is the variable called "Extract" (extractive capability of the governments). But even here, without considering the other factors that may be involved, it is not clear whether this could usefully serve as a policy variable. As for prediction, the author consistently talks of the "predictive" power of the regressions, but the question that naturally comes to mind is: prediction of what? This is a cross-section study, using all the 50 states. Prediction is obviously not meant for a new state that

*Assistant Professor of Economics, City College of the City University of New York.

might come into existence! For any of the existing states, to predict for a future year, it would be certainly unwise to ignore time series relationships in looking for a good forecasting model. Moreover, although this point may be subjective, a regression with an R^2 value as low as .68 (or even .75) may not be very satisfying for prediction purposes; of course, one should not look at the R^2 value as such, but should rather see how narrow a confidence interval we can get for the predicted value. (Incidentally, all the R^2 values reported in the paper are significant at the .01 level, as one may easily verify. But this only means that the hypothesis $R^2 = 0$ is rejected).

But as an exploratory study in an area where little has been done before, and as an attempt to provide a rationale for the observed differences in the governmental expenditures for education in the different states, the paper is highly successful and is extremely interesting and illuminating. The author has given us valuable insights into the possible determinants of higher and lower education expenditures by the governments.

For an exhaustive discussion such as is contained in this paper, there is little need for any outside comment. The other points which come to mind on reading the paper are but minor: (1) Only the simple linear forms have been used for the regression equations, and it is worthwhile trying other forms, as the author intends to do in the future. A more powerful predicting model may emerge from such an investigation, apart from helping to test the alternative rationale the author proposes at the end of the paper.

(2) One wishes that the author had given also the standard errors of the regression coefficients, instead of merely indicating which coefficients are significant. This would enable one to have a better appreciation of the coefficients. (3) It is not clear whether an intercept term was included in the regressions. (4) No mention is made of the presence or absence of multicollinearity; one hopes there was no multicollinearity. (5) The author ranks the regressor variables as the best, the second best, etc. If he is judging by the size of

the corresponding regression coefficients, are not these coefficients dependent upon the units of measurement?

This is a very valuable study, and further investigation in this area should be rewarding.

2

Enrollments in Vocational Education Programs — A Cross State Analysis

M. O. Clement and Alan L. Gustman*

Vocational education programs in the public schools are an important source of trained manpower. In 1970 there were almost nine million persons enrolled in these programs, more than double the number for 1960.[1] While enrollments in vocational programs —either on a full-time or part-time basis—constitute a substantial fraction of total public school enrollments, the proportion of public school students who are enrolled in vocational programs varies widely from state to state.[2] Our purpose in this paper is to present a number of reasonable explanations for this variation and to test the validity of these explanations. These tests are based on enrollment statistics collected from various sources for 1962, the last year for which a complete set of required data is available. For explanatory variables, however, other years, roughly coeval with 1962, sometimes had to be utilized.

We have not disaggregated our study to analyze vocational enrollments by type of program (e.g., agriculture), but have left consideration of this added dimension of choice to later study. We also have not disaggregated our analysis to separate the effects of various factors on full-time enrollments from their effects on part-time enrollments. There are not sufficient data on expenditures by type

*Dartmouth College. The research in this paper was supported by the U.S. Office of Education under Grant Number OEG-1-71-0107(508). We would like to thank our colleagues, George B. Pidot, Jr. and Martin Segal, for their helpful comments, and Jonathan H. Winer and Irene King for their able research assistance.

of enrollment to permit this kind of analysis. It is fortunate in this case that grouping full-time and part-time enrollments together does not present too serious a problem. The reason is that for vocational programs the distinction between the full-time and part-time students is not always a useful one. First of all, many programs encourage or require those who are enrolled to work. For example, those who enroll in distributive programs (i.e., programs that teach merchandising, marketing, or management) must be employed part-time to qualify for enrollment. Second, a major purpose of these programs is to encourage drop-outs to return to school on a part-time, if not on a full-time, basis and to provide post-high school vocational training for those students who have either made mistakes in planning their high school careers or who for other reasons would like to attend the vocational courses. Thus from a policy viewpoint those who are obtaining a vocational education on a part-time or post-high school basis are no less important than those who are attending on a full-time basis.[3] Nevertheless, we realize that careful disaggregation in further study may well serve to improve upon the estimates arrived at here.[4]

The Enrollment Decision

An individual of school age faces a large number of options in deciding upon the kind of schooling that he or she wishes to obtain. Among these, choices must be made with respect to how much education to obtain and what kind of education is best. Those who elect to enroll in a vocational program will in general have decided not to pursue a four-year college degree and will also have limited their expected occupation to those for which formal training is offered in the public schools.

The choice that each student and/or student's family makes among the alternative courses of study will depend upon the returns that are expected from each course—as determined in accordance with his or her background, current circumstances, and the nature of the job market that the student expects to face—the nature of the student's preferences with respect to the specific occupations for which training is offered, the utility value of the particular classes normally associated with each educational choice, and upon the quality of the various programs in the schools that are accessible to the student.

A number of authors have attempted to measure the returns to a high school education over dropping out of school and the returns to a college over a high school education.[5] These differences in returns are apparently substantial and are not too strongly influenced by differences in either the cognitive ability or the socio-economic background of the student.[6] Despite the fact that the returns to education—at least through the completion of four years of college—are substantial for those of different socio-economic backgrounds and of different ability levels, students from the lowest socio-economic backgrounds obtain less education. Thus, it seems that in addition to considerations pertaining to the returns to education, family related preferences and motivation, as well as the financial situation of the family, are likely to play an important role in shaping the education decisions of its members.[7]

The subject of returns to vocational, as opposed to other types of school programs, has also been studied extensively. In general it appears that at least in the years immediately following high school graduation there are positive returns to vocational education over comprehensive education for those who do not go on to college.[8] Moreover, and this is of particular importance to recent secondary school graduates who have faced a difficult time obtaining employment, there is evidence that the probability of unemployment is substantially lower for vocational program as compared with comprehensive program graduates. In addition, vocational program graduates apparently find their initial jobs much more quickly than do graduates of other high school programs. These findings seem to apply to both male and female vocational school graduates and to white and non-white graduates.[9] Together with available evidence which indicates that those who are enrolled in vocational programs are from families with lower socio-economic positions and are students who score poorly on examinations that measure the standard cognitive skills,[10] these findings of positive returns to those trained in vocational programs reinforce the popular notion that vocational training ("learning a trade") is a reasonable strategy for those who do not wish to continue their education beyond high school, and in particular that the strategy is sound for those students from poorer backgrounds and for those with lower cognitive ability. In addition, with more opportunity for (and at times the requirement of) part-time work for those enrolled in vocational programs, the burden of forgone earnings is lessened. This will provide further encouragement for enrollment in vocational programs for those from poorer families.

In sum, then, the findings of current research are consistent with the view that investment considerations, family background, and preferences are important elements in the answers to two basic educational questions: What determines the amount of education that an individual obtains? What determines the type of educational program that an individual enrolls in? It seems reasonable that in some cases the answers to these questions are arrived at sequentially—e.g., first a decision is made not to attend college, then a decision is made to obtain a vocational education—while in others the decision is made simultaneously by picking an ultimate occupation which implies a certain level and type of training.[11] Whatever timing sequence is followed, however, it is apparent that differences in investment opportunities and in family backgrounds should prove to be important considerations in explaining differences in vocational enrollments across states.

At the margin the decision to follow a particular educational course in high school is also likely to be influenced by the relative "quality" of the various educational programs that are available to the student's learning and eventually on his or her income quality—as measured by spending and the amount of real resources of different types used in the education process—on student performance, and eventually on earnings, indicates that these effects have been modest at best.[12] While it is conceivable that smaller class size and the availability of more individualized instruction and more modern facilities have a higher pay-off in terms of student learning for those who are enrolled in vocational education courses than for those in a standard educational course of study, we cannot be sure that the returns to higher spending on vocational programs are not in fact quite modest. However, even if the actual returns to differences in the "quality" of vocational programs—as measured by spending—are indeed small, vocational enrollments may nevertheless respond to differences in the quality of these programs. For one thing, parents and students may not be aware that program spending differences may have little effect on the student's learning and eventually on his or her income prospects.[13] For another, smaller classes and better equipment may increase the "consumption value" of a vocational education. In evaluating the likelihood that higher spending on vocational programs will make them more attractive to students, one should consider the fact that despite indications of only modest returns to differences in the overall quality of school programs, it has been found that at least in urban areas, public school enrollments appear to be responsive to differences in school quality.[14]

The Empirical Specification

Our discussion of the factors that influence students' choices of amount of schooling and of school program stresses the potential importance of the roles that are played by both the returns to education and by other factors in shaping the students' basic attitudes toward schooling. Thus the discussion leads us to the following groupings of factors which we believe are likely to account for the variations in vocational enrollments across states: (1) differences in the characteristics of the programs offered within the schools of each state; (2) differences in the socio-economic characteristics of the population of the states; (3) racial and ethnic differences among the populations of the states; (4) differing geographic characteristics of the states; and (5) differences in the occupational and industry mix of the jobs in the labor markets of the states. We deal with each of these factors in turn.

School Characteristics

In our study, six variables fall under the rubric of "school characteristics." These constitute the first set of explanatory factors for variations, across states, in the ratio of enrollment in vocational courses to overall public school enrollment (V EN/EN). These variables are: the amount of current spending on vocational programs per full-time public school student (V SP/EN); total current expenditures per student enrolled in public school (SP/EN); the percentage of public school students enrolled in high school (HS); the ratio of public school enrollment to the population in the state between the ages of 5 and 19; the average enrollment rate per operating school district; and the per capita expenditures on higher education in the state.

The first of these variables, the amount of spending on vocational programs per public school student (V SP/EN), is expected unambiguously to have a positive impact on relative enrollments in vocational programs.[15] By holding total spending per public school student (SP/EN) constant in a multiple regression, V SP/EN will provide a measure of the net enrollment consequences of the relative quality of the vocational education programs.[16] This variable, however—in what may be termed an "availability effect"—is also likely to serve as an index for the availability of vocational education programs in the school districts within a state. For while a low level for vocational spending per public school student for a particular state may reflect the fact that per student spending is low on the average for each vocational program offered, it may also reflect the fact that in many areas of the state no vocational programs are offered at all.[17] As more programs are offered in states with higher total spending on vocational programs, one would expect this "availability effect" to lead to a positive estimate of the effect of vocational spending on vocational enrollments. The data that are available from the Office of Educaton do not provide a direct measure of the "availability effect," e.g., average distance that must be travelled to enroll in a vocational program.[18] Thus, we are unable to isolate directly the difference in vocational enrollment that results from the drawing power of higher quality programs (what may be termed the "quality effect") from the difference in enrollment that results from the "availability effect." We do, however, present indirect evidence on the relative importance of these two effects below.

At this point it should be noted that if the relationship between V EN/EN and V SP/EN is specified to be linear in logs, the results may be readily transformed to indicate the effects of variations in spending on vocational education per student enrolled in *vocational* programs on relative enrollments in vocational programs.[19]

One more complication must be recognized in the relationship between vocational expenditures per public school student and relative vocational enrollments. Causality may not run simply from spending on vocational programs to enrollments in these programs.

While there is evidence that total school budgets in any given locality are relatively fixed in accordance with community wealth, demands for other community services, and the level of factor costs—and that these total educational budgets are then used to educate as many students as happen to enroll in the public schools[20]—there is still the possibility that expenditures on vocational programs may increase somewhat with expansion in vocational enrollments. If the empirical relationships were estimated with ordinary least squares (OLS) the effect of such simultaneous interactions would be to bias the estimate of the impact of vocational spending variations on vocational enrollments. We estimate our empirical relationships with both ordinary least squares (OLS) and with instrumental variable (IV) regression techniques.[21]

For a number of reasons, we have no firm *a priori* expectations concerning the direction of the effects of variations in the other "school characteristic" variables on relative vocational enrollments. Consider first the possible impact of changes in the amount of spending on all educational programs per full-time public school student (SP/EN), vocational spending per public school student constant. On the one hand, a substitution effect would lead to the prospect of a negative impact of higher values of this variable on relative vocational enrollments. On the other hand, more spending on other programs may mean a greater variety of educational programs offered within the school system. As a result, with no well defined alternative to a vocational course, students who elect a vocational program may not feel that they will be contrasted as sharply with their peers who are enrolled in academic programs as might be the case if few alternatives to the vocational program were available. Therefore, students may be more willing to participate in a vocational program in systems where spending on other programs is high. If the substitution effect is weak while the availability of a variety of other programs provides a stimulus to vocational programs, the coefficient of SP/EN in equation (1) could turn out to be positive.[22]

Two of the remaining school related variables—the proportion of public school students who are in high school (HS) and the public school enrollment rate per school age child in the population—may also exhibit either a positive or a negative relationship to relative vocational enrollments. The effects of a higher public school enrollment rate will depend upon relative preferences between vocational and other courses of the student who is marginal to the school system. If those who enroll in vocational courses are more committed to schooling than those in general educational courses, and the marginal students are most likely to fluctuate between dropping out of school entirely or enrolling in a general program, then areas with higher enrollment rates may exhibit a smaller proportion of students in vocational programs.[23] However, given the low socio-economic standing and cognitive ability of those in vocational programs,[24] the finding of a positive effect of higher enrollment rates on relative vocational enrollments would also seem to be reasonable.

Analogously, the relationship of the percent of total enrollment that is in high school (HS) to relative vocational enrollments may be positive or negative. That is, to the extent that variations in relative high school enrollments reflect the decisions of high school drop-outs and potential drop-outs at the margin, they will have similar impact to that of variations in the enrollment rate per school age child on vocational enrollments. In contrast, however, variations in the percent high school variable that merely reflect differences in the specific age structure of the school age population would be expected to have a systematic positive relationship to vocational enrollments. This, of course, is due to the fact that the vocational programs are offered at the high school level.

Next on the list of school related variables is the public school enrollment rate per operating school district. This variable has been included in an attempt to standardize for the effects of economies of scale and of a larger potential educational menu in larger school districts on the choice of an educational program. The relationship between this variable and relative vocational enrollments will depend upon whether the economies of scale and greater range of choice are more important for vocational or for standard educational programs.[25]

Lastly, on the premise that ready access to institutions of higher education will raise relatively the pay-off to a college preparatory program, and perhaps also will, through a kind of demonstration effect, alter preferences in favor of going on to college, we include per capita current expenditures on higher education in the state as an independent variable. The relationship of this last variable to vocational enrollments might, at first glance, be presumed to be negative. However, if the effect of more students making long-run educational plans is to create an atmosphere where community disapproval of dropping out of school is strong, and if those who stay in school because of this pressure have a high propensity to elect vocational programs, then the expected negative effect of greater spending on higher education on relative vocational enrollments may be reversed.

Socio-Economic Characteristics

We have discussed above the relationship between socio-economic characteristics and enrollment in vocational education programs. This discussion leads us to expect that higher levels of income in a state and higher levels of adult education will, *ceteris paribus,* be accompanied by lower levels of vocational enrollments. The specific measures of socio-economic level utilized in the statistical analysis are personal income per capita in each state (INC), the proportion of families in the state with income below $3,000, and the median level of education for those in the state who are 25 years of age or older. Our *a priori* expectation is that the elasticity of the relative vocational enrollment rate with respect to income and with respect to the levels of education will be negative, and that the elasticity of relative vocational enrollments with respect to the proportion of poor families will be positive.

Racial and Ethnic Characteristics of the Population

Holding income in the community and parental education constant, one might expect a relation between relative vocational enrollment and the racial mix of the population, if race is explicitly or implicitly considered as a factor in enrolling students in vocational programs. For example, in the "Fleishman Report" it is alleged that minority group students have been arbitrarily placed into vocational programs without regard to their wishes or talents.[26] On the other hand, the opposite tendency on the part of school officials has also been reported.[27] To test for systematic effects of racial mix within the community on relative vocational enrollments, we included the percentage of the population in each state that is non-white (NW) as an explanatory variable for relative vocational enrollments.

In the United States, the most frequent educational alternative to the public school system is that provided by parochial schools.[28] Religious affiliation clearly dominates many families' preferences for private education. Thus, it is likely that areas with large agglomerations of people in a faith which supports private schools are more likely to offer private educational alternatives. Relative tendencies to enroll in private institutions will have a systematic relationship to the proportion of relative vocational enrollments, if those students who are attracted into the private schools would have had a greater or lesser tendency than the average public school student to enroll in vocational courses. We have no *a priori* expectation as to the direction of this effect. Nevertheless, given its potential importance we included measures of proportion of the population that is Catholic (CATH) and the proportion of the population that is Jewish as independent variables in our estimating equation. These are two religious groups that heavily support their own educational facilities.

Geographical Characteristics

With imperfect labor mobility, one would expect that a job market must be of some minimum efficient size before it is possible to justify offering a wide variety of vocational education programs. Two variables which may provide a measure of this effect are the absolute population size of a state and the proportion of the population that is living in urban areas (URB). The importance of these measures may be increased if it is not only a minimum-size job market, but also, as noted in our discussion of the "availability effect," a minimum enrollment level that is required before a wide variety of vocational programs can be offered. Our expectation, therefore, is that these variables will be positively related to relative vocational enrollments in a state.

Labor Market Characteristics

The largest single group of independent variables in the estimating equation measures the occupational mix and industry mix of the jobs in each state. Given the fact that vocational programs are aimed at training students to fill particular jobs, one would expect that, if vocational students behave rationally, vocational enrollments will be higher where the job mix is more favorable to the employment of a vocational school graduate. The first of the variables that measures the job mix within a state is the proportion of employed workers in white collar occupations (WC). While some white collar jobs require higher levels of education, others involve a number of office and technical skills that may be learned in vocational schools. However, the major vocational programs for training in office skills were established following the enactment of the Vocational Education Act of 1963, and thus had little impact on vocational enrollments for our sample. It seems likely, therefore, that the larger the fraction of the employed persons in a state that are in white collar occupations, the smaller will be the relative vocational enrollments.

We also expect that where skilled jobs are plentiful, vocational enrollment will be encouraged. In contrast, a predominance of unskilled and perhaps service jobs will discourage vocational enrollment. Thus we include the proportion of employed persons in skilled, unskilled (UNS), and service occupations as independent variables.

The variables which measure the industry mix of the jobs in a state are the ratio of employment in manufacturing (MAN), wholesaling, and agriculture (AGR) to non-agriculture employment. We believe that a larger fraction of employment within a state in each of these sectors will lead to higher relative vocational enrollments. Kaufman noted a strong tendency for vocational graduates to be employed in manufacturing industries.[29] Wholesaling bears a special relationship to the distributive programs in vocational education, and obviously farm employment and agricultural programs are strongly related.[30]

The final independent variable is unemployment in the state. The possible effects of unemployment are ambiguous. We suspect that the relative advantages for a vocational graduate in competing with a comprehensive program graduate for a job are greater in a slack, rather than in a tight, labor market. Thus, on the one hand, if unemployment is expected to continue at a high level, vocational enrollments would seem to be encouraged. On the other hand, to the degree that job prospects for all high school graduates are dimmer when unemployment is high, students may stay in school longer and consequently be encouraged to enroll in non-vocational programs with their stronger linkages to opportunities for higher education.[31]

Empirical Estimation

We have cited a possible 22 explanatory variables which may account for variations in the relative enrollments in vocational programs across the 48 contiguous states for 1962. The precise sources for these variables are listed in the appendix. The basic form of the estimating equation is given by

(1) $\ln(V\ EN/EN) = \ln \alpha + \sum_{i=1}^{22} \beta_i \ln X_i + \epsilon,$

where X_i for $i = 1$ to 22 represent the 22 independent variables mentioned above and ϵ is a normally distributed error term.

In our discussion we have grouped the 22 variables into five categories. These categories relate, in turn, to the characteristics of the schools; the socio-economic characteristics of the population; the racial and ethnic composition of the population; geographic characteristics of the state; and the occupational and industry mix of the jobs in the state. Our expectation is that many of the variables within each of the groups will be collinear. Also, in some cases the expected direction of the impact of the independent variables on relative vocational enrollments is in doubt on theoretical grounds. Thus, there is reason to believe that a number of variables within each of the groups will exhibit coefficient estimates that are very small when compared to their standard errors. To deal with this problem we decided to serially eliminate those variables within each group for which the coefficient estimates are less than their corresponding standard errors.

We noted above that the relative vocational enrollment variable may have some simultaneous impact on the measure of relative spending on vocational education (V SP/EN) and on total spending per public school student (SP/EN). To allow for this possibility we estimate equation (1) with ordinary least squares procedures, and then also with instrumental variables using two sets of instruments.[32] The first set of instruments consists of 27 variables. These instruments include the remaining 19 variables in equation (1), along with a set of exogenous variables that are known to strongly influence the amount of spending on education per public school student[33] and two variables that measure the relative amounts of state and federal aid to vocational programs. It is of interest to note that these instruments are the same as those that would be utilized to estimate the structural equations of a simultaneous equations system with the two-stage least squares estimating technique, where spending per public school student, relative spending on vocational education programs, the public school enrollment rate, and relative vocational enrollments were the jointly determined endogenous variables. The second set of instruments differs from the first in that the measures of state and federal aid to public schools as a whole and the proportion of aid to vocational programs have been eliminated on the ground that these variables may be endogenous to the system.[34] For the same reason this second set of instruments does not include the variable which measures per capita expenditures on higher education in the state.

Empirical Results

The empirical estimates of equations are presented in Table 1. As promised above, those variables that exhibited coefficient estimates that fell consistently below their standard errors were eliminated from the regression equations. The estimates in the first column have been obtained from an ordinary least squares regression, while those in the second and third columns are based upon regressions which utilize the instrumental variables technique with the sets of instruments described above. Since the regression equation

Table 1

Empirical Results*
(t=statistics in parentheses)

Variable	OLS	IV-1	IV-2
V SP/EN	0.73 (6.79)	0.67 (5.26)	0.52 (2.87)
SP/EN	0.71 (1.93)	0.55 (1.18)	0.64 (1.18)
HS	−0.70 (−1.13)	−0.59 (−0.87)	−0.58 (−0.78)
INC	−1.10 (−2.66)	−1.02 (−2.19)	−1.06 (−2.05)
NW	−0.04 (−1.02)	−0.04 (−0.87)	−0.04 (−0.80)
CATH	−0.18 (−3.12)	−0.17 (−2.63)	−0.19 (−2.56)
URB	1.04 (3.15)	1.03 (2.92)	1.00 (2.57)
WC	−0.98 (−1.51)	−0.92 (−1.30)	−1.03 (−1.31)
UNS	−0.75 (−1.96)	−0.78 (−1.90)	−0.87 (−1.91)
MAN	0.27 (2.17)	0.28 (2.05)	0.28 (1.87)
AGR	0.13 (1.55)	0.13 (1.47)	0.11 (1.18)
CONST	4.28 (1.14)	4.23 (1.04)	5.17 (1.13)
$\bar{R}^2$	.75	.71	.65
S.E.	.2167	.2310	.2544

*V SP/EN: Current spending on vocational programs per full-time student enrolled in public elementary and secondary schools.
SP/EN: Total current expenditures of public elementary and secondary schools per student enrolled.
HS: High school enrollment as a percentage of public school enrollment.
INC: Personal income per capita.
NW: Percent of population that is non-white.
CATH: Percent of population that is Catholic.
URB: Percent of population that lives in urban areas.
WC: Percent of employed persons in white collar occupations.
UNS: Percent of employed persons in unskilled occupations.
MAN: Ratio of manufacturing employment to non-agricultural employment.
AGR: Ratio of farm employment to non-agricultural employment.
CONST: Constant term in the regression equation.
V EN/EN: Dependent variable. Ratio of vocational enrollment to total public school enrollment.

was specified to be linear in logs, all coefficient estimates may be interpreted as measuring elasticities at the point of means.

From the results in Table 1 it can be seen that estimates for only about half of the variables that were discussed above are reported. The others that we suspected might have systematic relationship to vocational enrollments had little discernible statistical impact and consequently were eliminated from the regression equation. Each of the five major groups is, however, represented among the eleven remaining variables.[35]

The effects of the variables which pertain to "school characteristics" are all consistent with our theoretical reasoning. The high positive coefficient of vocational spending per public school student implies that students enroll at a higher rate in higher quality vocational programs and/or that the "availability effect" is operative —that is, that higher spending on vocational education is an index of the availability of vocational programs throughout a state. The use of instrumental variables slightly lowers the estimated size of the elasticity of vocational enrollment with respect to vocational spending. Nevertheless, the estimated elasticity remains above 0.5 and exceeds two standard errors in value.

In our discussion above, we said that the finding of a positive effect of spending per public school student (V SP/EN constant) on relative vocational enrollments would be expected if the substitution effect between vocational and other programs is weak and, at the same time, in places where a greater variety of other educational programs are offered, students feel that there is less of a stigma attached to the choice of a vocational program. Unless the stimulating effect of a greater availability of choice in nonvocational programs on vocational enrollments is more substantial than seems reasonable on *a priori* grounds, this finding implies that the substitution effect between vocational and other programs in response to quality differences is probably quite weak relative to the availability effect. This in turn would lead us to believe that the positive correlation of the two variables—the ratio of vocational to total enrollments and vocational spending per public school student—with the availability of vocational programs probably is the most important factor determining the size of the coefficient of V SP/EN in Table 1.[36]

The finding of a negative coefficent for the percent high school variable may imply more of a tendency for students who are marginal to the high schools to choose general over vocational programs than is the case for other students. However, the coefficient estimate for this variable is small enough relative to its standard error that we cannot be sure that its sign is in fact "correct." Parenthetically, the same comment may also be applied to the coefficient estimated for the SP/EN variable discussed above.

As for the other measures of school characteristics, the fact that their coefficient estimates were below their standard errors in value means that we have no evidence that cross-state differences in public school enrollments per school age population, differences in average school district size, or differences in per capita expenditures on higher education have systematic relation to relative vocational enrollments for the states.

Of the variables that pertain to the socio-economic status of the population of each state, only per capita personal income (INC) has a sizeable impact on relative vocational enrollments. The measures of poverty and of the education of the adult population in the state added little in the way of explanatory power. The negative elasticity of vocational enrollments with respect to per capita personal income is as expected. It is consistent with the observations referred to previously of substantial returns to those who complete high school vocational training programs, as compared to those who terminate their education after completing a standard high school course of study, and with the inverse relationship between parental income and their children's education.

Our findings indicate a very weak negative relationship between the proportion of the population that is non-white (NW) and relative vocational enrollments. This would lead us to believe that there are no consistent differences between non-whites and whites in terms of admission to vocational programs. This may reflect the fact that discrimination in these admissions is not very widespread. On the other hand, it may possibly mean that the way of discriminating varies from area to area in accordance with particular circumstances. Thus, in some areas non-whites may be shuttled onto the vocational track, while in others, perhaps where vocational training is more highly valued, non-whites may be excluded. This suggests the possibility of interaction effects between the percent non-white variable and a number of other independent variables. However, given the number of observations and the number of variables already included in the study, we did not test for these effects.

One measure of the ethnic composition of a state's population appears to have important relationship to relative vocational enrollments. That measure is the percent of the population that is Catholic (CATH). The finding of a negative relationship here may imply that the students who attend parochial schools would have a greater tendency to enroll in vocational programs were they to attend public schools, than do the students who currently attend public schools. A more straightforward interpretation would be that Catholics have weaker preferences for vocational education. We have no evidence that would allow us to choose between these two alternatives.

The finding in Table 1 of a positive relationship between urbanization of the population (URB) and relative vocational enrollments is consistent with the view that the availability of a large number of different jobs within an area increases the attractiveness of vocational programs, perhaps facilitating specialization in program offerings. We did not find, however, that the absolute size of a state's population had a similar effect.

The results for the remaining four variables, all of which pertain to the mix of jobs in the labor market in the state, are consistent with our *a priori* expectations. In labor markets where white collar and unskilled jobs are more numerous, vocational enrollments are apparently discouraged. On the other hand, in labor markets where the manufacturing and agricultural sectors are important sources of employment, relative vocational enrollments are likely to be higher. The availability of skilled, or service jobs, or jobs in wholesaling had little discernible statistical relation to relative vocational enrollments. Moreover, vocational enrollments did not vary systematically in accordance with the unemployment rate in a state.

Summary and Conclusion

In this paper we have attempted to identify the factors that are of importance in explaining interstate variations in the ratio of enrollments in vocational education programs to the overall level of public school enrollments. Available evidence seems to indicate that for those who terminate their education upon receiving a high school degree, vocational education yields higher returns than does a standard high school program. If students enroll in vocational programs because of the returns to such programs in the job market, and if some careers lend themselves to vocational training more than others, one would expect to observe that vocational enrollments are sensitive to the job mix within a state. We found this to be the case. For example, vocational enrollment is higher in states where manufacturing is important and lower in states where unskilled jobs are prevalent. Other factors of importance in shaping vocational enrollments include urbanization and the proportion of Catholics in the population. The former factor has a positive impact on vocational enrollments; the latter a negative one. Moreover, as expected, in states where income is higher, and thus students are more likely to continue schooling beyond the high school level, vocational enrollments are found to be lower. Lastly, our results indicate a consistent positive relation between relative vocational enrollments and spending on vocational programs per public school student in the state. Although this relationship may be explained either in terms of the effects of relative quality of vocational programs on enrollments or in terms of the correlation of vocational spending and enrollments with the availability of vocational programs throughout a state, the evidence that we were able to muster points toward the importance of the "availability effect."

We recognize, of course, that the years since the implementation of the 1963 Vocational Education Act have witnessed enormous changes in the variety of vocational education programs offered, in the funding for these programs, and in the kind of labor market that the vocational education graduate encounters. For this reason, and because of the highly aggregative nature of our analysis, it is not likely that the elasticity estimates presented in our empirical analysis will be useful for precise planning of current policy. Nevertheless, we have every expectation that further analysis with 1970 data (when they become fully available) will tend to support our qualitative findings which do have implications for broad policy questions that pertain to the planning of vocational education programs.

On the whole, these findings imply that enrollments in vocational programs vary as they would if students were attempting to maximize their income and employment prospects given their family circumstances, current preferences, and available opportunities. To be sure, some of this behavior may in large part reflect the results of planning and persuasion on the part of those who administer vocational programs. However, given what we know about the current state of such planning,[37] and the fact that our data pertain to the very beginning of the Kennedy-Johnson era, with its considerable emphasis on manpower plannning, much of the observed enrollment behavior is likely to be due to the planning efforts of the students themselves. Therefore, in our view these findings add weight to the arguments of those who believe that, given reasonable amounts of information, students enrolled in public schools under a voucher type plan—where students are permitted to choose among a variety of educational programs and schools—will in fact make reasonable and rational choices among broad program differences that will work to the benefit of the student. Certainly, none of our findings is inconsistent with this viewpoint.[38]

An additional implication is that the supply-side response of vocational students to differences in labor market conditions is a factor that should be considered in planning vocational programs. In that way vocational schools would be less likely to encounter situations where there is either an excess supply of applicants to vocational programs or an excess of vacancies in these programs. Also, recent changes in the nature of the public school population, e.g., the continuing closing of parochial schools, may have predictable but non-proportional effects on potential enrollments in vocational programs. Careful planning requires that these effects be taken into account.

NOTES

1. U.S. Office of Education, *Digest of Educational Statistics,* 1971, p. 36.

2. In 1962, the year for which we conduct our statistical analysis, the ratio of total vocational enrollments to public school enrollments averaged about 10 percent. The coefficient of variation for observations for the forty-eight contiguous states is 41 percent. We deflate the vocational enrollments by the total number of full-time primary and secondary public school students because we wish to avoid explanations that would be unduly influenced by population differences.

3. See U.S. Office of Education, *Vocational and Technical Education, Annual Report,* Fiscal Year 1966, p. 11, for an outline of the policy goals of the Vocational Education Act of 1963.

4. The available data do not permit disaggregation on the basis of type of school in which the vocational program is offered. It is of interest to note that in 1965, of the 16,890 schools that offered vocational programs, 15,741 of the schools were regular or comprehensive secondary schools. The remainder were mainly secondary and post-secondary vocational schools and community or junior colleges, with a few (70) universities and colleges offering vocational programs. U.S. Office of Education, *Vocational and Technical Education, Annual Report,* Fiscal Year 1965, p. 35.

5. The basic reference work in the area remains G. S. Becker, *Human Capital,* New York, 1964. A series of carefully derived estimates of the rates of return to schooling for whites and non-whites is given in G. L. Hanoch, "An Economic Analysis of Earnings and Schooling," *Journal of Human Resources* (Summer, 1967), pp. 310–29.

6. In addition to Becker, *op. cit.,* ch. 4, see, for example, P. J. Taubman and T. J. Wales, "Higher Education, Mental Ability and Screening," *Journal of Political Economy* (January/February, 1973), pp. 28–55; J. C. Hause, "Earnings Profile: Ability, and Schooling," *Journal of Political Economy* (May/June, 1972), Part II, pp. S108–38; and C. Jencks *et al., Inequality: A Reassessment of the Effect of Family and Schooling in America,* New York, 1972.

7. For a discussion of the relationship of parental socio-economic status to the parents' educational aspirations for their children and to their childrens' education aspirations, see J. N. Morgan, M. H. David, W. J. Cohen, and H. E. Brazer, *Income and Welfare in the United States,* New York, 1962. The relationship of school enrollments to parental socio-economic status is examined in J. Conlisk, "Determinants of School Enrollment and School Performance," *Journal of Human Resources* (Spring, 1969), pp. 140–57. Jencks *et al., op. cit.,* contains extensive analysis of the relationship of socio-economic background to student performance, and to earnings in later life. See also S. Bowles, "Schooling and Inequality from Generation to Generation," *Journal of Political Economy* (May/June, 1972), Pt. II, pp. S219–51 and the following comments.

The theoretical framework for analyzing the effects of differences in the availability of funds on the optimal investment in human capital is presented in G. S. Becker and B. R. Chiswick, "Education and the Distribution of Earnings," *American Economic Review* (May, 1966), pp. 358–69.

R. C. Young, W. V. Clive, and B. E. Miles claim, among others, that given the job market situation that he faces and the pressures for income at home, the drop-out's decision to leave school is in many cases a rational one. *Vocational Education Planning, Manpower Priorities and Dollars,* Columbus, 1972, pp. 83–85.

8. T. Hu, M. L. Lee, and E. W. Stromsdorfer, "Economic Returns to Vocational and Comprehensive High School Graduates," *Journal of Human Resources* (Winter, 1971), pp. 25–50. A. J. Corrazzini, "The Decision to Invest in Vocational Eduction: An Analysis of Costs and Benefits," *Journal of Human Resources, Supplement, Vocational Education* (1968), pp. 59–87.

9. Hu, Lee, and Stromsdorfer, *op. cit.,* pp. 36, 37, and 46.

10. R. N. Evans and J. D. Galloway, "Verbal Ability and Socio-economic Status of 9th and 12th Grade College Preparatory, General and Vocational Students," *Journal of Human Resources* (Winter, 1973), pp. 26, 28, and 30. Evans and Galloway find that about 70 percent of those enrolled in vocational education programs are in the bottom two quartiles of the Project Talent socio-economic index. They also find that over 70 percent of the males who are enrolled in vocational programs and over 60 percent of the enrolled females scored below the median on Project Talent General Ability Profile.

11. For a discussion of occupational choice for high level manpower, see R. B. Freeman, *The Market for College Trained Manpower,* Cambridge, 1971. In his empirical analysis Freeman finds that enrollments in courses leading to entry into various occupations respond to changing economic circumstances in those occupations. The lags that he finds in the system are consistent with those implied by theoretical considerations pertaining to the kind of formal training required for each field.

12. See, for example, J. S. Coleman *et al., Eqaulity of Educational Opportunity,* Washington, D.C., 1966. Despite what appear to be justified methodological criticisms [e.g., as pointed out in S. Bowles and H. M. Levin, "The Determinants of Scholastic Achievement—An Appraisal of Some Recent Evidence," *Journal of Human Resources* (Winter, 1968), pp. 3–24] the basic conclusions of the "Coleman Report" seem to be holding up well to further analysis, as in F. Mosteller and D. P. Moynihan (eds.), *On Equality of Educational Opportunity,* New York, 1972; and C. Jencks *et al., op. cit.*

13. In fact, parents and students were almost certainly not aware of this prospect in 1962. The attention of social scientists has been strongly focussed on this issue only since the release of the "Coleman Report" in 1966.

14. A. L. Gustman and G. B. Pidot, Jr., "Interactions Between Educational Spending and Enrollments," *Journal of Human Resources* (Winter, 1973), pp. 3–23.

15. Two things should be noted about the relative vocational spending variable. First, spending on vocational programs is deflated by total full-time public school enrollments for the same reason that vocational enrollments are deflated by this measure; that is, to avoid explanations that would be unduly influenced by population size differences. Second, data on capital utilized in vocational education programs which would be compatible with our sample are not available. Although an investment series is available for later years, it is not of sufficient duration to permit one to calculate the capital utilized in the vocational education process. Thus we

have confined our analysis to the effects of measures of *current* educational spending on enrollments.

16. An important dimension of quality is the amount of choice among the different kinds of vocational programs that is available to the students in each school. Increased choice will often entail greater expense, but is likely to result in greater relative vocational enrollments. On the matter of how much choice is in fact available in vocational programs, see J. J. Kaufman, "The Role of Education in the Transition from School to Work," in A. R. Weber, F. H. Cassell, and W. L. Ginsburg (eds.), *Public-Private Manpower Policies*, Madison, 1969, p. 201.

17. This possibility is made more likely by the fact that our data pertain to 1962, and therefore the strong impetus to the construction of vocational schools under the 1963 Vocational Education Act had not yet been realized. (See U.S. Office of Education, *Vocational and Technical Education, Annual Report*, Fiscal Year 1966, pp. 5–7.) For a discussion of the absence of vocational education programs in the school districts of many states, see p. 12 of the publication cited above. On this point, see also J. J. Kaufman, *op. cit.*, p. 194.

18. There is recent survey evidence of substantial travel by students to obtain vocational training. This travel is generally from rural areas to small cities, small cities to suburbs, and suburbs to larger cities. E. R. Kay, *Vocational Education: Characteristics of Teachers and Students, 1969*, Washington, D.C., 1970, p. 14.

19. By definition, spending on vocational education per public school student (V SP/EN) is equal to the product of spending on vocational education per student enrolled in vocational programs (V SP/V EN) and the ratio of enrollments in vocational programs to overall public school enrollments (V EN/EN). In logarithmic terms, if the relationship between relative vocational enrollments and total spending on vocational programs per public school student is given by

$$\ln (V\ EN/EN) = \ln \alpha + \beta \ln (V\ SP/EN),$$

then

$$\ln (V\ EN/EN) = \frac{1}{1 - \beta} \left[\ln \alpha + \beta \ln (V\ SP/V\ EN) \right].$$

Given this convenient result, as well as the fact that coefficient estimates obtained with a log-log regression represent direct measures of elasticities, the empirical relationships specified and estimated throughout the paper are all linear in logs.

20. Gustman and Pidot, *op. cit.*

21. It would be useful to present the OLS based estimates even if we were certain that simultaneous equations bias was a serious problem. For in a small sample the variance of an OLS estimator is less than that of an estimator that is based on instrumental variables. As a result the OLS estimator may turn out to be the closest to the true parameter value. For further explanation, see A. S. Goldberger, *Econometric Theory*, New York, 1964, p. 360.

22. For reasons similar to those stated on page 12, the statistical relationship between total spending per public school student and relative vocational enrollments will be estimated with ordinary least squares and with instrumental variables.

23. Such a result would be consistent with the findings of M. K. Taussig for New York City schools. Specifically, Taussig states: ". . . the vocational program in New York City has demonstrated no over-all significant holding power over potential dropouts." See "An Economic Analysis of Vocational Education in the New York City High Schools," *Journal of Human Resources, Supplement, Vocational Education* (1968), p. 82. For evidence on drop-outs by course of study, see J. Combs and W. W. Cooley, "Dropouts: In High School and After School," *American Educational Research Journal* (May, 1968), pp. 343–63.

24. See Evans and Galloway, *loc. cit.*

25. These economies, to the degree that they are realized in school size rather than in school *district* size, are not accounted for here.

26. The New York State Commission on the Quality, Cost and Financing of Elementary and Secondary Education, *Report*, Vol. 2 (1972), pp. 7.32–7.33.

27. Young, Clive, and Miles, *op. cit.*, pp. 108–10.

28. Ninety-six percent of all students enrolled in non-public elementary schools and 89 percent of all students enrolled in non-public secondary schools are found in church-related institutions. U.S. Department of Health, Education, and Welfare, Office of Education, *Digest of Education Statistics* (1969 edition), p. 29.

29. J. J. Kaufman, "Occupational Training Needs for Youth," *Journal of Human Resources, Supplement, Vocational Education* (1968), p. 129.

30. Measures of employment in other sectors were tried in preliminary regression runs and were found to have little systematic relationship to relative vocational enrollments.

31. To the extent that cross-sectional variation in unemployment rates measures structural differences in labor markets rather than the relative importance of deficient demand unemployment for the labor markets of the different states, the above discussion may not apply.

32. There is also an outside possibility that two variables, the ratio of public school enrollments to the school age population and the percent of public school students who are in high school (HS), may be influenced by relative vocational enrollments. We estimated versions of equation (1) where these variables were also treated as endogenous. This had little effect on our results.

33. The additional set of variables is from Gustman and Pidot. These variables were used to explain variations in per student spending in public schools for a set of urban areas (*op. cit.*, p. 8). They include measures of teachers' salaries, property values, measures of the mix between residential, commercial, and industrial property, and measures of state and federal aid. These variables are defined more precisely in the appendix where the appropriate sources are also given.

34. For a discussion see, for example, J. S. Osman, "Dual Impact of Federal Aid on State and Local Expenditures," *National Tax Journal* (December, 1966), pp. 362–72.

35. The t-statistics for the estimates obtained with instrumental variables are reported to facilitate a rough comparison of coefficient estimates with the corresponding standard errors. The small sample distributions of the instrumental variable estimators are not known. In addition, coefficients of determination may turn out to be misleading indicators of goodness of fit in an equation where there is simultaneous interaction between the dependent and independent variables. For this reason, the $\overline{R}^2$'s reported here must be interpreted with care. For further discussion, see R. L. Basmann, "Letter to the Editor," *Econometrica* (October, 1962), pp. 824–26.

36. In his comments on this paper, Professor Silver suggests, we think quite reasonably, that the positive sign of the coefficient of SP/EN in Table 1 may reflect the correlation of this variable with the availability of vocational education within a state. Thus, the "availability effect" may influence the coefficient estimates for both spending variables and obscure measurement of the substitution effect between vocational and non-vocational programs.

37. For a discussion of the content of vocational education and its response to changes in the labor market, see G. G. Sommers, "The Response of Vocational Education to Labor Market Changes," *Journal of Human Resources, Supplement, Vocational Education* (1968), pp. 32–58. The subject of planning vocational education programs is discussed extensively in Young, Clive, and Miles, *op. cit.*

38. A voucher plan for vocational education is recommended in The New York State Commission on the Quality, Cost and Financing of Elementary and Secondary Education, *op. cit.*, pp. 7.42–7.44.

APPENDIX
The Data

I. The Dependent Variable

V EN/EN: Ratio of vocational enrollment to total public school enrollment (1961–62). Sources [9, p. 21; 11, pp. 40–41].

II. The Independent Variables (from Table 1)

V SP/EN: Current spending on vocational programs, (by all governments for federally reimbursed programs and functions) per full-time student enrolled in public elementary and secondary schools (1961–1962). Sources [9, p. 26; 11, pp. 40–41].

SP/EN: total current expenditures of public schools, per student enrolled in public elementary and secondary schools (1961–1962). Source [11, pp. 55–56, 40–41].

HS: high school enrollment (grades 9–12) as a percentage of total public school enrollment (1961–1962). Source [11, pp. 40–41].

INC: personal income per capita (1962). Source [4, p. 8].

NW: Percent of the population that is non-white. Source [5, p. I–164].

CATH: percent of population that is Catholic (1950 data, and estimates based on 1936 data). Source [2].

URB: percent of population that lives in urban areas (1960 data). Source [6, p. 2].

WC: percent of all employed persons, 14 years and over, in occupations classified as "white collar" (1960 data). Source [5, p. I–227].

UNS: percent of all employed persons, 14 years and over, in occupations classified as "unskilled" (1960 data). Source [5, p. I–227].

MAN: ratio of manufacturing employment to total non-agricultural employment (1963 data). Sources [6, p. 6; 1, p. XXXI].

AGR: ratio of farm employment to total non-agricultural employment (1963 data). Sources [7, p. 443; 1, p. XXXI].

III. Other Variables Employed in the Analysis

Ratio of total public school enrollment (1961–1962) to the number of persons ages 5 through 19 in the state (1960 data). Sources [11, pp. 40–41; 5, pp. I–167 to I–172].

Percent families with income less than $3,000 (1959 income of 1960 families). Source [6, p. 3].

Median years of school completed, persons 25 years and older (1960 data). Source [6, p. 3].

Population density per square mile (1962 data). Source [4, p. 8].

Population 1962. Source [4, p. 8].

Average public school enrollment rate per operating school district (1961–62). Source [11, pp. 29, 40–41].

Current expenditures on higher education (1961–1962) per capita (1962 population). Sources [10, p. 88; 4, p. 8].

1950 population that is Jewish (1953). Source [2].

Average annual salary of instructional staff in public schools (1961–1962). Source [11, p. 70].

Expenditures on vocational education from federal sources (FY 1962) as a percentage of revenue receipts of public elementary and secondary schools from federal sources (1961–1962). Sources [9, p. 26; 11, p. 53].

Expenditures on vocational education from state sources (FY 1962, for functions and programs aided by the federal government only), as a percentage of revenue receipts of public elementary and secondary schools from state sources (1961–1962). Sources [9, p. 26; 11, p. 53].

Estimated market value of all taxable property per capita (1961). Source [3, Tables 13, 2; 4, p. 8].

Percent of the gross assessed value of locally assessed taxable real property that is not commercial or industrial (1961). Source [3, pp. 34–35].

Revenue receipts of public elementary and secondary schools from the state government per capita (1961–62). Sources [11, p. 53; 4, p. 8].

Revenue receipts of public elementary and secondary schools from the federal government per capita (1961–62). Sources [11, p. 53; 4, p. 8].

Percent of all employed persons, 14 years and over, in occupations classified as "skilled" (1960). Source [5, p. I-277].

Percent of all employed persons, 14 years and over, in occupations classified as "skilled" (1960). Source [5, p. I–277].

Ratio of wholesale trade employment to non-agricultural employment (1963). Sources [6, p. 9; 1, p. XXXI].

Unemployment rate: total, average for 1962, as a percentage of the total work force. Source [8, p. 279].

Sources of Data

1. Bureau of Labor Statistics, *Employment and Earnings Statistics* (various years).
2. National Council of Churches of Christ in the U.S.A., *Churches and Church Membership in the U.S.*, 1956–58, Series A, No. 2, Table 2, and No. 3, Table 4.
3. U.S. Bureau of the Census, *Census of Governments*, 1962, Vol. 2, *Taxable Property Values*.
4. U.S. Bureau of the Census, *Census of Governments*, 1962, Vol. 7, *State Reports*, Nos. 1–50, "Selected Items for Comparison with Other States".
5. U.S. Bureau of the Census, *Census of Population: 1960*, Vol. I, *Characteristics of the Population*, Part 1, U.S. Summary.
6. U.S. Bureau of the Census, *County and City Data Book, 1967*.
7. U.S. Department of Agriculture, *U.S. Agricultural Statistics: 1964*.
8. U.S. Department of Labor, *Manpower Report of the President: A Report on Manpower Requirements, Resources, Utilization and Training*, March, 1970, p. 279.
9. U.S. Office of Education, *Digest of Annual Reports of State Boards for Vocational Education to the Office of Education*, Fiscal Year 1962.
10. U.S. Office of Education, *Digest of Educational Statistics, 1966*.
11. U.S. Office of Education, *Statistics of State School Systems 1961–62* (Circular No. 751).

*Comments on "Enrollments in Vocational
Education Programs—A Cross State Analysis"*

Morris Silver*

Clement and Gustman have written a paper of value to economists
interested in expanding the range of application of demand (or
choice) theory and perhaps to educational policy-makers as well.

The central question examined is whether and how strongly the
decision of a public high school student (or his family) to follow a
vocational rather than a general educational program is influenced
by the relative "quality" of the alternative types of program. In
multiple regressions for states "holding constant" current expenditures of public elementary and secondary schools per student enrolled (SP/EN), the relative quality of vocational programs is measured
by current vocational educational expenditures per student in public elementary and secondary schools (VSP/EN). Putting aside a
number of qualifications it is found that the ratio of vocational to
total enrollment increases reasonably sharply and reliably with increases in relative vocational program quality: the point elasticities
with respect to VSP/EN vary from .52 to .73 while the corresponding t-statistics vary from 2.87 to 6.79 (the highest in the study).

An excellent feature of the research is the use of instrumental
variable procedures. This is done to take account of the possibility
that causality runs not only from relative expenditures to relative
enrollment, but from relative enrollment to relative expenditures.
The latter channel of causation exists because school officials may
accommodate to autonomous shifts in the composition of student
demand by reallocating their budgets—i.e., if the demand for vocational programs increases, funds may be shifted into them in order
to maintain the level of quality.

That increases in relative expenditure on vocational programs
are accompanied by increases in relative vocational enrollment
might actually mean that young persons shift from apprentice or
on-the-job type programs into high school vocational programs or

*Professor of Economics, City College of the City University of New York.

even worse that academically oriented students drop out to enter private schools in response to increased stress on vocational programs in the public high schools. However, the cogency of such interpretations is lessened by the inclusion in the regressions of "high school enrollment as a percent of public school enrollment."

As pointed out in the paper, a substitution effect would lead to a negative coefficient for total spending per student (SP/EN). I find totally unconvincing the authors' attempt to "explain" the finding of a positive (but not statistically significant) coefficient on the ground that "more spending on other programs may mean a greater variety of educational programs offered within the school system" with the result that "students feel that there is less of a stigma attached to the choice of a vocational program." Fortunately, in an earlier version the authors more plausibly suggest that the positive coefficient reflects an "availability effect"—i.e., that in areas where *total* expenditure per student is relatively low, vocational programs are less likely to be available in the high schools. If the facts were to demonstrate such a relationship, the inclusion of SP/EN in the regressions would actually help to standardize the results for differences in availability. Consequently the case for viewing the coefficient of VSP/EN as a measure of the response to differences in relative quality would be strengthened.

Clement and Gustman are able to employ only current expenditure data. How serious is the absence of capital estimates when we are dealing with the quality of vocational programs? Is it possible that, in part, higher current expenditures might represent an (inadequate) attempt by school officials to compensate for a lack of capital equipment? If so, higher current vocational expenditures would less clearly reflect the quality of vocational programs.

No evidence is presented on the extent of collinearity problems in the equations. But surely equations including income, a measure of the extent of poverty, and race as variables must be considered suspect. One crude but simple indicator of harmful multicollinearity is whether there are any simple correlations among the independent variables exceeding the entire equation's multiple correlation coefficient.

Only unweighted logarithmic regressions are presented. Variables whose coefficients "fell consistently below their standard errors were eliminated from the regression equations." If experiments with other forms took place, this should be noted somewhere in the paper. Some reference might also be made to the econometric literature dealing with the procedures for choosing among alternative specifications and tests for heterosedasticity (e.g., Durbin-Watson). Finally, I must enter the caveat that it is a good idea to make as many decisions regarding variables included in the regressions *before* they are run.[1]

NOTE

1. In this connection see Michael C. Lovell and Edward Prescott "Multiple Regression with Inequality Constraints: Pretesting Bias, Hypothesis Testing and Efficiency," *Journal of the American Statistical Association* (June, 1970), pp. 913–25 and T. A. Bancroft, "On Biases in Estimation Due to the Use of Preliminary Tests of Significance," *The Annual of Mathematical Statistics,* 15 (1944), pp. 190–204.

3

Can Increased Spending Improve Our Schools?
Dogma vs. Causal Analysis

Morris Silver*

The urgent learning problems of underprivileged youngsters taken together with serious budget problems of state and local governments in recent years have contributed to a resurgence of research interest in the factors determining the learning performance of primary and secondary school students. Some of the findings have been interpreted to mean that increases in expenditures for school inputs (e.g., instructional supplies and equipment, teacher experience and schooling) have little or no effect on performance (e.g., see [4, p. 316]). There is even the implication that smaller classes (an important form of increased input) have a negative effect on performance. Given the unexpected nature of such interpretations and given the vested interests of harried city officials seeking to satisfy competing demands for funds, enemies of Civil Service "merit systems" for teacher selection, groups wishing to radically alter the educational process, and advocates of racial integration, it is not at all surprising to find them bursting into the public media and beginning to reshape public opinion.[1] In certain influential intellectual circles the view that better schools cannot be obtained by spending more on them appears to be approaching the status of an unchallengeable dogma. But what if the dogma isn't true?

*Professor of Economics, City College of the City University of New York. I am indebted to Robert Leiter and Benjamin Klebaner for their helpful comments and encouragement.

In reality the relationship between school inputs and student performance is quite complex. Let us assume that student performance is a function of school and non-school inputs. Thus,

(1) SCORE = F(CLASS SIZE, A)

where:
"SCORE"(S) represents a measure of learning performance (e.g., a reading score);

"CLASS SIZE"(CS) *inversely* represents all school inputs;

"A" represents all non-school inputs including parent and student inputs and innate ability.

The issue being debated is the sign and magnitude of the coefficient of CLASS SIZE. Problems of interpretation arise because CLASS SIZE is not exogenous: in part it is determined by SCORE. This is so because in the *current real world* school and other public officials often allocate more school inputs to "educationally disadvantaged" students ("conpensatory inputs").[2] Sometimes public officials use (socioeconomic) proxy measures for SCORE to determine financial allocations to school districts and sometimes explicit measures of "educational deprivation" are considered. To cite some examples: (1) the formula used by the New York City Board of Education to determine the allocation of tax-levy funds to local school districts takes account of reading retardation; (2) reading retardation is also considered in distributing New York State Urban Education Funds to city school districts; (3) Federal Title I funds are distributed to school districts based on educational need. More generally, through their representatives, communities may raise or lower expenditures according to whether targeted performance levels are under or over achieved. This type of relationship may be represented by

(2) CLASS SIZE = G(SCORE, B)

where:

The coefficient of "SCORE" is taken to be positive;

"B" represents all other factors determining "CLASS SIZE" (e.g., income and wealth levels in a community, union contracts, whether more experienced teachers and administrators have the right to transfer from less to more preferred schools);

"B" is defined so as to make its coefficient negative."

In order to put the problem into clear focus I assume that:

(a)   The common sense view that reductions in Class Size will improve performance is true (i.e., the coefficient of "CS" is negative).

(b)   "A" takes only the values "low" and "high."

(c)   "B" is constant (or more realistically, variation in "B" is small relative to variation in "A").

It follows that the "S" curves in the figure are negatively sloped while the "CS" curve is positively sloped. In equilibrium both CLASS SIZE and SCORE will be higher in "high A" schools (i.e., S_1 is higher than S_0 and $(CS)_1$ is higher than $(CS)_0$). If SCORE is regressed on CLASS SIZE, the coefficient will (given my assumptions) be *positive* in spite of the fact that the S curve is negatively sloped.

It is plausible to expect that across school districts increases in socioeconomic status raise both A (via increased student-parent inputs) and B (via increased ability to purchase school inputs). The resulting positive correlation between A and B means that across districts as socioeconomic status rises not only the "S" but the "CS" curve will shift to the right. Consequently, the upward bias in the estimated coefficient of CS will be greater within than across school districts. This may well account for some very curious findings where the research was confined to particular centrally controlled and financed school systems.[3] In such districts a rise in socioeconomic status shifts the S curve but not the CS curve.

Further, if socioeconomic status is an important determinant of B as well as of A, studies such as the Coleman Report [4] and Burkheads' [2], which seek to measure the impact of school inputs after taking account of socioeconomic factors, intensify the difficulties of correctly estimating the coefficient of CS. This type of approach implicitly attributes the entire impact of socioeconomic factors to A.[4]

One possible solution to the problem of identifying the S curve is to assume that A can be held constant by running separate regressions of SCORE on CLASS SIZE for different socioeconomic groups. The usefulness of such an approach depends on the validity of this assumption and the extent of the remaining variation in B. Some studies of this type exist; they are consistent with the view that school inputs do make a difference.

1. Bowles and Levin [1] utilize Coleman Report data for Negro verbal achievement in grade 12 and conclude from their regression analysis that "Both teachers' salaries and a very imperfect measure of school facilities (presence of science labs) are significantly related to achievement. . . .The variable measuring teacher characteristics has a higher significance level than any other in the analysis, including the social background of the students."

2. Guthrie, Kleindorfer, Levin, and Stout [10] use Coleman Report data for a sample of Michigan 6th grade students. The students are classified into 10 different socioeconomic groups. For each of the 10 groups scores on reading, mathematics, and verbal ability tests are correlated (rank) with a number of school inputs. The expected signs and statistical significance are achieved by school site size, building age, percent of makeshift classrooms, lib-

rary volumes per student, supply of textbooks, classrooms per 1,000 students, teachers' experience, and teachers' verbal ability,

3. Hanushek [11] uses Coleman Report data to regress school average verbal scores of white and Negro 6th grade students in the Metropolitan North on a variety of school inputs. For both whites and Negroes the coefficients of teacher experience (years) and teacher verbal ability are positive and statistically significant.

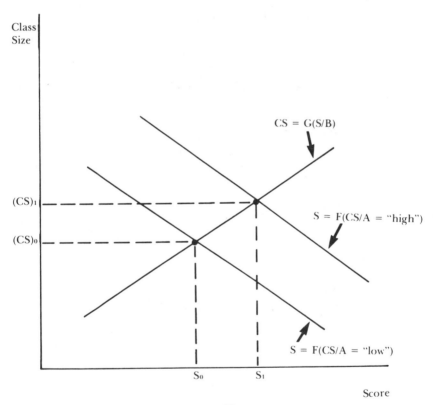

Figure

4. Kiesling [13] utilizes New York State data for 97 school districts. He regresses the average achievement score in basic subjects for students with similar socioeconomic backgrounds on net per-pupil expenditures for school inputs. The coefficient of expenditures fluctuates in sign (a majority are positive), but some of the positive values do achieve statistical significance. Kieslings's results show symptoms of serious multicollinearity problems and his decision to deflate expenditures by average daily attendance makes school inputs seem larger in districts with higher absence rates.

5. Utilizing Project Talent data for 12th grade males of low socioeconomic origins, Ribich [15] observes a positive relationship between achievement levels and school district expenditures per student.

6. The U.S. Commission on Civil Rights [17, p. 96] reports that within a given socioeconomic class there is a "pronounced relationship" between a composite index of teacher qualifications and 12th grade verbal achievement.

7. A recent study of the Baltimore City Public School system investigated the relationship between class size and pupil achievement holding constant parental occupation, race, curriculum, and the score on an intelligence test. The reported findings are striking [7, pp. 142–43]: (a) Students in smaller classes "made significantly greater gains. . .on both standardized reading and arithmetic tests over the. . .period 1959–1964 in 188 comparisons to 55 for students in larger classes—a 3.4 to 1 ratio in favor of smaller classes. . ."; (b) "Out of 192 comparisons, pupils in the smallest class size grouping [1–25 students] made significantly greater gains. . . in a ratio of 7.3 to 1"; (c) "The advantages of the smallest class size (1–25) were considerably [greater] for nonwhite than for white students."

8. In the above studies the unit of observation is the individual student. More Effective Schools (MES) in New York City provides evidence for *entire schools* of given socioeconomic status. The MES have below average class sizes, team teaching (four regular teachers to every three classes), and four or five Assistant Principals in contrast to the usual one or two. It is found that ghetto MES children have perceptibly higher reading scores than either control group

children or the general population of ghetto school children (see [8]. [14], and [16]).

One may believe in school "reform" without basing it on the argument that how much we spend on schools simply doesn't matter. It is ironical that if the dogmatists win the minds of the public, researchers may be once again able to observe the "traditional" relationship between school inputs and outputs. A correct interpretation of the significant findings to date, however, does not permit the conclusion that spending less will not affect adversely the educational outcome.

NOTES

1. Roger Freeman of Stanford University has recently angrily criticized the editors of the New York Times [5] for daring to suggest, against "the overwhelming research evidence," that we spend more on our schools. He has also informed the readers of the Wall Street Journal [6] that: "The absence of a positive cost-quality relationship. . .between class size, teachers' salary or experience, age or type of facilities and pupils learning achievements was conclusively demonstrated six years ago in the massive Coleman report. Findings of a four-year reanalysis by Daniel P. Moynihan. . .diminish further the extraordinarily weak influence which school 'inputs'. . .seem to have on educational 'outputs'."

2. See Cain and Watts [3].

3. In studies of the Chicago, Boston, and the English school systems Burkhead [2], Katzman [12], and the Plowden report [9] observe *positive* relations between measures of the student-staff ratio and measures of reading performance. According to Freeman [6] "An analysis of the New York City School Fact Book reveals [that] the reading skills of the students in the low-expenditure, large-class, schools have averaged above grade level; in the high-expenditure, small-class schools below grade level."

4. See Bowles and Levin [1].

REFERENCES

1. Samuel Bowles and Henry M. Levin, "More on Multicollinearity and the Effectiveness of Schools," *The Journal of Human Resources,* Vol. III, No. 3 (Summer, 1968), pp. 393–400.

2. Jesse Burkhead, *Input and Output in Large-City High Schools* (Syracuse, N.Y.: Syracuse University Press, 1967).

3. Glen G. Cain and Harold W. Watts, "The Controversy About the Coleman Report: Comment," *The Journal of Human Resources*, Vol. III, No. 3 (Summer, 1968), pp. 389–92.

4. James S. Coleman, *Equality of Educational Opportunity* (Washington D.C.: Office of Education, U.S. Department of Health, Education, and Welfare, 1966).

5. Roger A. Freeman, Letter to the Editor, *New York Times*, March 25, 1972.

6. ———, *Wall Street Journal*, March 31, 1972.

7. Orlando F. Furno and George J. Collins, *Class Size and Pupil Learning* (Baltimore City Public Schools, 1967).

8. Harry Gottesfeld, "More Effective Evaluation for More Effective Schools," *The Urban Review*, Vol. 2, No. 6 (May, 1968), pp. 15–34.

9. Great Britain Central Advisory Council for Education (England), *Children and Their Primary Schools*, Vol. 2, Appendix 4 (London: Her Majesty's Stationery Office, 1967).

10. James Guthrie, "A Survey of School Effectiveness Studies," in *Do Teachers Make A Difference* (Washington D.C.: Bureau of Educational Personnel Development, Office of Education, U.S. Department of Health, Education and Welfare, 1970), pp. 25–54.

11. Eric A. Hanushek "The Education of Negroes and Whites" (unpublished Ph.D. dissertation, Department of Economics, Massachusetts Institute of Technology, 1968).

12. Martin T. Katzman, "Distribution and Production in a Big City Elementary School School System," *Yale Economic Essays*, Vol. 8, No. 1 (Spring, 1968), pp. 201–56.

13. Herbert J. Kiesling, "Measuring a Local Government Service: A Study of School Districts in New York," *Review of Economics and Statistics*, Vol. XLIX, No. 3, (August, 1967), pp. 356–67.

14. Harry L. Miller and Roger R. Woock, *Social Foundations of Urban Education* (Hinsdale, Ill.: Dryden Press, 1970).

15. Thomas I. Ribich, *Education and Poverty* (Washington D.C.: Brookings Institution, 1968).

16. Sidney Schwager, "An Analysis of the Evaluation of the MES Program Conducted by the Center for Urban Education," *The Urban Review*, Vol. 2, No. 6 (May, 1968), pp. 15–34.
17. U. S. Commission on Civil Rights, *Racial Isolation in the Public Schools*, 2 Vols. (Washington D.C.: U.S. Government Printing Office, 1967).

4

On the Irrelevance of Educational Opportunity Costs

Charles R. McKnew, Jr. and David G. Tuerck*

I. Introduction

The literature on human capital has produced a criticism of the manner in which public expenditures on education are financed. According to this criticism, the public sector does not account for the earnings and other opportunities which students forgo in order to attend school. Such "educational opportunity costs" are said to impose as real a fiscal burden as any explicit outlay for teachers, janitors, or chalk. Yet they are ignored:

> Although most economists include earnings foregone as a cost in analyzing the rates of return to investment in education, such costs are not taken into account in educational planning. Nor do earnings foregone appear in official educational statistics. It is fair to say that, in determining educational policy, in authorizing programs, and in allocating resources to finance education, we go on ignoring earnings foregone although they are well over half the real cost of higher education.[1]

Implicit in this criticism is the idea that "educational planners"

*The authors are, respectively, Assistant Professor of Economics and Research Associate, the Regional Research Institute, West Virginia University, and Research Economist, the Center for International Business, Pepperdine University, Los Angeles. Mr. Tuerck completed his work on this paper while he was Associate Professor of Economics, California State College, Bakersfield. The authors wish to thank Professors Richard A. Bilas, James M. Buchanan, Charles J. Goetz, and Richard D. Auster for their helpful comments. Any errors remain the responsibility of the authors.

should "account" for educational opportunity costs by determining the total amount of such costs that are incurred: "The important thing is that some reasonable convention be adopted that will include student time as part of the aggregate costs of the schooling that has become embodied in the population." The measure of cost used under this convention will have both predictive and normative value, being adaptable "for use in theories that seek to explain, interpret and predict behaviour in diverse institutional settings" and for use "as a tool for prescriptive purposes in societal decision-making."[2]

We shall argue that existing measures of educational opportunity cost[3] are in fact not useful for predicting student behavior or for societal decision-making. However "aggregated," such measures lack scientific content because they are, as we shall say, "choice-influenced" rather than "choice-influencing." They are irrelevant to any "planner" who allocates resources to finance education.

We first explore a comparative static model of student choice in which certain, alternative measures of educational opportunity costs are identified and compared. In that context, we examine next the alleged relevance of such costs to educational opportunity and to student behavior. We conclude with some observations about educational planning and about educational opportunity costs as social costs.

II. A Comparative Static Model of Student Choice

Let a student receive a total income i equal to the sum of his earned income ei and his unearned income ui. Earned income is equal to a fixed wage rate wr multiplied by the amount of time he allocates to work, and unearned income equals some fixed income he receives irrespective of how he allocates his total time between competing uses. Total income may be taken as a composite for commodities purchased by the student under relative price constancy.

The student divides his total time between non-work time nwt and work time wt. Non-work time is a composite good[4] which he divides between education time et and leisure time lt. Education time is defined to include time allocated to school attendance and to the so-called at-home complements to school attendance such as reading and studying. Tuition charges, interest charges on educational loans, and the returns to given amounts of education time are assumed to remain constant.

Now let the student define a continuously differentiable, quasi-concave utility function $U = U(i, u)$, where $u = u(et, lt)$, and let him maximize U subject to $tt = \dfrac{i - ui}{wr} + lt + et$. His choice calculus may be illustrated in Figure 1, where indifference curves between i and nwt appear in the left-hand graph and indifference curves between et and lt appear in the right-hand graph.[5] For example, suppose that his indifference maps include curves U_1 and u_1, that he receives an unearned income of zero, and that he works at a wage rate of OM/OL. He will then adjust simultaneously to point Z on LM, at which $\dfrac{\partial U}{\partial i} \Big/ \dfrac{\partial U}{\partial nwt} = \dfrac{1}{wr}$, and to point I on $C'B$, at which $\dfrac{\partial u}{\partial et} \Big/ \dfrac{\partial u}{\partial lt} = 1$. He will receive a total income of OG and consume OC units of non-work time, of which he allocates $O'A$ to education and AI ($= AB$) to leisure.

It may be observed that the student's wage rate is the "marginal opportunity cost" of education time and that this marginal opportunity cost enters (along with unearned income) into the determination of his behavior: the student forgoes earnings equal to his wage rate for each hour he allocates to education time (or leisure time), and this opportunity cost affects his allocation of total time between work, education, and leisure.

However, we have seen that opportunity costs are supposed to be "aggregated" or added up in order to be useful:

> It is precisely when major social decisions are under consideration that the need for an opportunity-cost approach becomes most urgent. . . .The opportunity-cost approach has thus been used. . .in planning models that specifically included comparisons among alternatives viewed in large lumps.[6]

Let us therefore assume that there are *four* students who have adjusted to points Z and I along lines LM and $C'B$ in Figure 1. Then let the same four students receive unearned income endow-

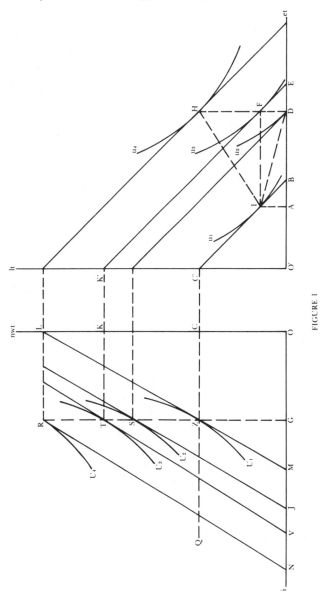

FIGURE 1

ments of zero, JM, VM, and NM. The first student remains at Z and I, as the others adjust to points S and D, T and F, and R and H, respectively. Total incomes remain constant at OG ($= NM$), the earned income of the first student remains constant at OG, and the earned incomes of the remaining three students adjust to NJ, NV, and zero. The first student holds his education time fixed at $O'A$, as the others expand theirs by the amount AD to $O'D$.

How do we measure the opportunity cost of the additional "lump" of time that each student thus allocates to education? According to one line of reasoning, "the concept of earnings foregone is cogent and precise." Opportunity costs should be computed by subtracting the earnings realized by a student from his "full earnings opportunity."[7] Applied to our four students, this definition yields measures of opportunity cost equal to zero ($= NM - NM$), JM ($= NM - NJ$), VM ($= NM - NV$), and NM ($= NM - $ zero).[8]

Alternatively, Professor Wiseman has argued that "the 'opportunity cost' of obtaining education is not just foregone earnings, but the sum of this and foregone leisure, somehow valued in money."[9] We may adjust our computations accordingly to obtain the following measures: zero ($=$ zero $+$ zero), VM ($= JM + VJ$), VM ($= VM + $ zero), and VM ($= NM - NV$). The educational opportunity costs of given lumps of time may thus be measured in different ways, depending upon whether or not leisure is accounted for.

However, from this example, it does not appear to matter how such costs are measured or, indeed, whether they are measured at all. In either case, we simply take some lump of the student's total time and multiply the amount of time contained in it by the wage rate. Though perhaps interesting for its own sake, the resulting product does not provide any information that may be used to prescribe fiscal policy or predict student behavior. Educational opportunity costs, so defined, do not determine the amount of time which a student allocates to education. Rather, they are determined *by* the amount of time he allocates to education as he adjusts to the wage rate and unearned income. They are "choice-influenced" rather than "choice-influencing."[10]

III. Educational Opportunity Costs and Educational Opportunity

Professor Lewis Solmon has argued that existing differences in educational opportunity costs pose a barrier to "equality of educational opportunity":

> The importance of opportunity costs arises because any amount (or percentage) of family income which must be foregone when a potential earner stays in school probably will hurt a poor family more (or in different ways) than will the same amount foregone by a wealthy family.
>
> The latter point is based on the assumption of diminishing marginal utility of income.[11]

On the basis of this reasoning, Solmon prescribes a system of "incentive payments for poor families to send their children to school." Such payments he says, "would reduce the differential influence of opportunity cost on the decision to enroll" and provide other inducements for the poor to expand their education time.[12] Prescription of this kind is difficult to fault simply because it can support so many interpretations. Nowhere does it answer the question, "Under what circumstances would the proposed policy succeed or fail if, in fact, it was adopted?" We might ask precisely what Professor Solmon means by "an incentive payment" to attend school. Is it a lump-sum subsidy which is equal to educational opportunity cost and which is paid only to poor students? Is it a subsidy to which some *quid pro quo* has been attached? Or is it a lump-sum subsidy which has been paid to rich and poor students alike in the hope that diminishing marginal utility of income would cause the poor students to receive larger subsidies than the rich? We explore these three possible interpretations here.

Lump-Sum Subsidies for the Poor

Consider the foregoing example, in which three students with positive income endowments allocate $O'D$ units of time to education, while a "poor" student with a zero income endowment allocates only $O'A$ units of time to education. We assume that equality of educational opportunity would require the poor student to expand his education time to $O'D$ and that educational opportunity cost is equal to the value VM of work and/or leisure time which this expansion of education time would cause him to forgo. Let us say that Solmon's proposal would "succeed" if VM is just equal to the amount of the smallest lump-sum subsidy which would induce the "poor" student to expand his education time by AD to $O'D$. Let us say that it would "fail" if VM is greater than this amount (so that a lump-sum subsidy less than VM would be sufficient to achieve the desired adjustment) or if it is less than this amount (so that a lump-sum subsidy greater than VM would be required to achieve the desired adjustment).

Suppose that the student would respond to a lump-sum subsidy equal to VM by moving along expansion paths ZR and IF to points T and F. Solmon's proposal would succeed. The student would be just willing to expand his non-work time by an amount equal to the desired expansion of education time, and he would be just willing to allocate all of his expanded non-work time to education. But this case is surely special and only by coincidence descriptive of actual behavior. Even under the highly simplified conditions assumed here, it is possible to identify an infinity of cases in which the proposed policy would fail.

Suppose, instead, that the student would respond to a subsidy equal to JM by moving along expansion paths ZR and ID to points S and D. Then Solmon's proposal would fail because this subsidy would be less than VM but large enough to achieve the desired effect. Since expansion path ZR represents the limiting case of a zero income-elasticity of demand for income, it provides only one such example in which the opportunity-cost subsidy is too large. Holding the student's right-hand expansion path fixed, a clockwise rotation of ZR around point Z would cause his preferences to represent a negative income-elasticity of demand for income. He would be willing to substitute additional non-work time for work time as he adjusted to an increase in unearned income, and the required subsidy would decrease in size.

Now suppose the student would respond to a subsidy equal to NM by moving along expansion paths ZR and IH to points R and H. The proposal would fail again because this subsidy would be greater than VM but just large enough to induce the desired adjustment. Still larger subsidies would be required if we held the right-hand expansion path fixed and allowed ZR to rotate in a counterclockwise direction around Z, so that the student's preferences represented a positive income-elasticity of demand for income. An infinity of such cases are possible in which income is a normal good and in which the student would substitute some additional earnings for non-work time.[13]

Subsidies with a Quid Pro Quo *Attached*

Perhaps Solmon would attach a *quid pro quo* to each incentive payment, such that a student would have to expand his education time by a given amount as a condition for receiving his payment. The government might wish to offer each student the smallest subsidy he would accept with the *quid pro quo* attached.

Consider a student at points Z and I in Figure 1, who has attained $U_1 = U(OG, u(O'A, AI))$, and let the government offer him a subsidy of VM (which we have accepted as a measure of opportunity cost) on the condition that he expand his education time to $O'D$. Barring any attempt on his part to game with the government for a larger subsidy, he would accept the *quid pro quo:* Since he could attain $U' = U(NV + VM, u(O'D, AI))$ and since $U' > U_1$, he could attain at least one position that he preferred to his original position at Z and I. As long as he preferred education time to work time and as long as he could satisfy the *quid pro quo* and still enjoy at least as much total income and at least as much leisure time as he did before, he would be better off to accept the subsidy and receive the additional education time.

Nevertheless, VM might not be the *smallest* subsidy for which he would satisfy the *quid pro quo*. A subsidy equal to VM permits him to increase his utility from U_1 to U' by expanding his education time to $O'D$ as he holds income and leisure constant. But, since he could attain U' by consuming as much income and leisure as he did at U_1, there may be some utility indicator U'' which also is greater than U_1 (though less than U') and which he could attain by consuming somewhat less income and/or leisure than before. In that event, the least-cost subsidy would be less than VM.

The opportunity-cost subsidy might be defended on the ground that it would not only achieve equality of educational opportunity but also provide windfall gains to students who are poor. But, if the purpose is to make poor students richer as well as better educated, then why not set the subsidy at some amount which is equal to two or three times opportunity cost or opportunity cost raised to a power of ten? Indeed, why restrict the subsidy to students when there are nonstudents among the poor who are equally deserving?

Further questions may be raised about students who refuse to satisfy the *quid pro quo*. Suppose that a student refuses to expand his education time to $O'D$, in the hope that the government will offer him a larger subsidy. Does he thereby forfeit his right to equality of educational opportunity, and, if not, what does opportunity cost have to do with the subsidy he finally does accept? Or suppose that the government offers him a subsidy and *quid pro quo* under which he could not attain as much total income and as much leisure as he had attained before. If he rejects the subsidy, there is no way to tell whether he simply prefers the *status quo* or whether he has decided to hold out for a larger subsidy. In that event, does the government abandon the student, the *quid pro quo,* or its opportunity-cost calculations?

Lump-Sum Subsidies for the Poor and the Rich

According to Solmon, diminishing marginal utility of income causes the opportunity cost of education to be greater for the poor than the rich. It may therefore follow that if all students, rich and poor alike, received lump-sum subsidies equal to opportunity cost, the poor would receive larger subsidies than the rich and, in that way, achieve equality of educational opportunity.

This interpretation can be evaluated by referring to Figure 2, where two students, Mr. Poor and Mr. Rich, have initial incomes of CZ and CV, respectively. We assume that the two students have identical preferences and that they allocate identical amounts of time to non-work *(OC* at the pre-subsidy point).[14] At his pre-subsidy point Z, the marginal utility of income for Mr. Poor is relatively high (as illustrated by the relatively high absolute value of the slope of his initial indifference curve U_{P1} at that point), and, at his pre-subsidy point V, the marginal utility of income for Mr. Rich is relatively low (as illustrated by the relatively low absolute value of the slope of his initial indifference curve U_{R1} at that point). Yet the

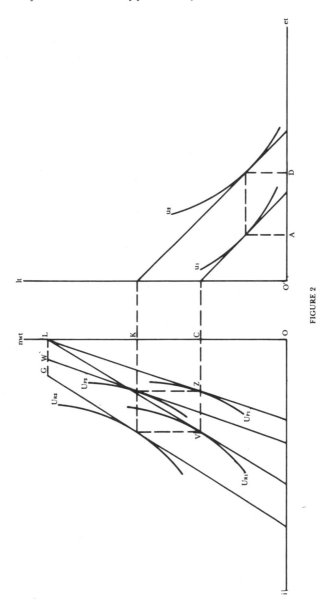

FIGURE 2

opportunity cost to Mr. Poor of expanding his education time by a given amount $AD = CK$ is less than the opportunity cost to Mr. Rich of expanding his education time by the same amount. If each student received a subsidy equal to his opportunity cost, Mr. Rich would receive a subsidy equal to GL while Mr. Poor received a subsidy equal to WL. Solmon's assumption of diminishing marginal utility of income fails to exclude an infinity of such cases in which educational opportunity costs are larger for the rich than the poor.

Solmon claims that his argument "is analogous to the argument for progressive taxation which asserts that in order to equalize the 'burden' of the tax, higher income groups should be taxed at *higher* rates than at the same rate as all groups."[15] However, Professor Musgrave has shown that it is impossible to defend the various "equal burden" theories of progressive taxation without arbitrarily circumscribing individual utility functions, even if we assume diminishing marginal utility of income. Furthermore, if we hold against interpersonal comparisons of utility, "the entire concept of equal sacrifice becomes so much nonsense and must be discarded—lock, stock, and barrel."[16]

IV. Educational Opportunity Costs and Prediction

The literature has produced a number of predictive theories that relate student behavior to the "supply and demand for human capital." We may relate these theories to our own model of student choice[17] by giving explicit consideration to interest rates and rates of return in the student's choice calculus. Let us observe that the student incurs costs in the form of interest rates on money that he borrows or on savings that he forgoes in order to allocate additional units of time to education. These interest rates will vary directly with the amount of time he allocates to education if, as we expect, "a person accumulating capital must shift from the cheapest, to the second cheapest, and on eventually to expensive sources."[18] The student may thus be said to have a positively-inclined supply schedule that relates interest rates to education time.

We next define the student's rate of return as that rate of discount which sets the present value of all future returns to education time equal to opportunity cost. The student expands his education time as long as, but only as long as, the rate of return exceeds the interest rate. Given that the rate of return varies inversely with the amount of time he allocates to education, we may say that the student has a negatively-inclined demand schedule that relates interest rates to education time. Supply equals demand when the student has distributed his total time between all uses in such a way that the rate of return to education equals the interest rate.

The Economist's Theory

It has been argued that changes in opportunity costs exert predictable effects on the demand for education time:

> Measurement of opportunity cost is an essential element in any analysis that would attempt to explain rates of persistence in school. As a first approximation, it might be considered to be the "economist's" theory. According to this theory, school continuation rates will rise, other things equal, when opportunity costs fall; continuation rates will fall when opportunity costs rise.[19]

Suppose that the student's supply and demand schedules are represented graphically, with the interest rate on the vertical axis and the amount of education time on the horizontal axis. According to "the economist's" theory, an increase in the student's wage rate would cause his whole demand schedule to shift downward and to the left as the rate of return to each amount of education time fell. Given the increased marginal opportunity cost of education time, he would have to discount the future returns to each amount of education time at a lower rate than before in order to set the present value of those future returns equal to opportunity cost. He would adjust downward along the fixed supply schedule as the equilibrium rate of interest and amount of time allocated to education by him decreased.

In fact, however, economic theory provides little basis for such reasoning. The demand for education time is a function not only of the interest rate, but also of total income. An increase in the student's wage rate will raise the cost to him of allocating an additional hour of time to non-work and will, on that account, cause him to substitute work time for education (and leisure) time. But it will also raise the total income he receives for allocating any given amount of time to work and will, on that account, cause him to expand education time (provided that education time is a normal good). The substitution effect of the increase in marginal opportunity cost will cause his demand schedule to shift down and to the left, but the income effect will cause it to shift up and to the right. "Which dominates cannot be determined *a priori.*"[20]

The theory cannot be salvaged, either, if we take the explanatory variable to be some measure of "aggregate" opportunity costs. As we have seen, such costs are endogenous, rather than exogenous, to the student's choice calculus ("choice-influenced," rather than "choice-influencing"). If we multiply the student's wage rate by the additional amount of time he allocates to (or away from) education, we may readily identify students for whom continuation rates vary directly with opportunity costs. For example, in our comparative static model of student choice, the three students who incurred positive opportunity costs did allocate additional time to education whereas the student who incurred a zero opportunity cost did not. Education time and opportunity cost varied directly as each student adjusted to his (positive or zero) unearned income endowment.

Opportunity Costs and Incomes

This brings to mind a somewhat different theory of student behavior. According to Solmon:

> Income levels should be a major determinant of the amount of education. When incomes in a state rise, opportunity costs of being in school rise and so the rate of return to any amount of schooling should fall. This would cause the demand curve to shift downward.[21]

We have already seen that variations in earned income will not exert predictable effects on the demand for education time.[22] However, we might give separate consideration to the effect which variations in unearned income are likely to exert on this demand. Because such variations occur, by definition, at constant wage rates, they exert income, but not substitution effects. If unearned income rises (and, again, if education time is a normal good), the demand schedule will shift upward, rather than downward. Marginal opportunity costs will remain constant, and positive aggregate opportunity costs will be incurred as additional lumps of time are allocated to education. Thus variations in unearned income appear to exert an effect which is just the opposite of that predicted by existing theories of student choice.

In rebuttal, it might be argued that our criticism stresses the "consumption components" of student choice, whereas it is the "investment components" that really matter.[23] But any such argument seems contradictory to the very notion of opportunity cost: If his wage rate is $2 per hour, the student chooses not between $2 worth of human capital and $2 worth of non-human capital but between (1) $2 worth of human capital and allocating an hour of time to education and (2) $2 worth of non-human capital and allocating that same hour of time to work. The consumption component is inseparable from the investment component.

Distributive Theories of Student Behavior

Some theories purport to explain why poor students allocate less time to education than rich students. For example, according to Professor Schultz:

> The increase in the value of time of students, as earnings rise with growth, obviously increases the student's cost of acquiring a college education. . . .For many students from families who are not rich, the supply implications of the rise in earnings foregone are real and harsh.[24]

Contrary to this reasoning, it may be observed that a rise in wage rates (marginal opportunity costs) makes the student better off by permitting him to enjoy more total income and/or non-work time. The effect of an increased wage rate is to cause him to adjust his allocation of total time between competing uses in such a way as to attain the greatest possible increase in utility. His demand for education time may either rise or fall with earnings, depending in part on the relative strength of the substitution and income effects which are exerted by the increase in the wage rate. But the increased opportunity cost at which the student allocates a unit of time to education does not impose any kind of burden on him: Rather, it shows the increased earnings which he would rather forgo than allocate that same unit of time to work.

Schultz has said that "opportunity costs provide a unified explanation" of the fact that "many talented children from low-income families do not continue their schooling beyond the age that is legally compulsory."[25] If by "opportunity costs" he means "wage rates," then he might be construed to say that income effects are stronger than substitution effects: If the wage rates received by poor children increased, their demand schedules for education time would shift upward and they would continue their education beyond the legally compulsory age. If, on the other hand, he means "aggregate opportunity costs," then, as we know, it is the student's decision to allocate more or less time to education that explains opportunity costs, not the other way around.

By their very nature, aggregate opportunity costs cannot explain why rich students allocate more time to education than poor students. It is no more "interesting to note"[26] that attendance rates vary inversely with aggregate opportunity costs divided by income than it would be to note that aggregate opportunity costs divided by income vary inversely with attendance rates. Neither statement provides any explanation of student behavior.

The "Imperfection-of-the-Capital-Market" Theory

Professor Albert Fishlow has commented as follows upon the observed relative preponderance of rich students in American high schools at the turn of the century: "In no small measure it was the imperfection of the capital market, which prevented persons from borrowing to invest in themselves, that led to this discrimination. Only those who could self-finance their opportunity costs could afford education."[27]

Poor students may have higher rates of time preference for income than rich students and, on that account, allocate less time to all forms of non-work, including education. But if existing "imperfections" in the capital markets were removed, students in general could borrow to finance additional education and additional leisure. The effect on their allocation of time and on the nature of any "discrimination" would depend in part on their rates of return to education and rates of time preference for leisure. In order for the imperfection-of-the-capital-market theory to hold true, poor students would have to have sufficiently high relative rates of return to education and sufficiently low relative rates of time preference for leisure that they would allocate more additional time to education, on the average, than rich students. Otherwise, the continued existence of capital-market imperfections would seem to discriminate more against the rich than against the poor. Contrary to Professor Fishlow, the mere existence of such imperfections does not guarantee the existence of any discrimination against the poor. His theory is weakened by evidence that poor students enjoy lower rates of return to education than rich students.[28]

V.   Educational Opportunity Costs and "Educational Planning"

It is sometimes difficult to tell whether fiscal choice is misinformed because it does not account for educational opportunity costs or whether educational opportunity costs are important because it does. On the one hand, Professor Schultz complains that "it is simply impossible to plan efficiently when over half of the real costs are treated as 'free' resources" and that "educational planners receive no signals that the value of the time of students is rising relative to material inputs." According to him, "there is no search for ways of economizing on the time of students."[29]

On the other hand, according to Becker, "the increased awareness of the importance of forgone earnings has resulted in several attempts to economise on students' time, as manifested, say, by the spread of the quarterly and tri-mester systems."[30] Indeed, according to Solmon, educational administrators and faculties have been aware of educational opportunity costs all along: "In the nineteenth century, to minimize opportunity costs, particularly in rural areas, school was set up so classes conflicted with work opportunities as little as possible."[31]

These opposing views rest on the common assumption that the

social cost and the opportunity cost of education time are the same. However, it may be shown that these costs are not the same and that, insofar as the former is relevant, the latter is not.

We define marginal social cost as the smallest payment for which a person would allocate one more hour of time to a given activity, and we define marginal social value as the largest payment which anyone would be willing to offer that person to allocate one more hour of time to the activity. We also assume that an "efficient" plan or price system would cause a person to allocate additional time to any activity for which marginal social value exceeded marginal social cost. Suppose, then, that a person would be willing to allocate one more hour of time to wine-tasting for $2 even though he could earn $5 by allocating that same hour of time to garbage-collecting. The marginal social cost of his wine-tasting time would be $2, not $5. If the marginal social value of wine-tasting time was $4, an efficient plan or price system would "signal" him to allocate additional time to wine-tasting (and less time to garbage-collecting and/or leisure).

Similar reasoning applies to the case in which a person allocates time to education as well as to work and leisure. The marginal social cost of education time is the smallest payment for which a person would be willing to allocate one more hour to it. In particular, if a student would allocate one more hour of time to education for a payment as small as zero, then the social cost of that hour of education time is zero (which is to say, it is "free" to society) even if its opportunity cost to him is positive.

The opportunity-cost calculations which are said to represent "over half the real cost" of education are therefore misleading: Students allocate their time between competing uses in such a way that the (positive, negative, or zero) payment they do receive for allocating an hour of time to any activity is equal to the smallest payment they would have to receive for allocating an hour of time to that activity. But as long as they prefer education time to work time, in the sense that they would have to receive a smaller payment in order to allocate an hour of time to education than they would have to receive in order to allocate that same hour of time to work, the payment they do receive for an hour of work time will be greater than the payment they would have to receive for an hour of education time. The opportunity cost of an hour of education time will be greater than its social cost. An efficient plan, which accounts for social cost, will therefore ignore educational opportunity cost, as planners may already understand.

VI. Conclusion

We have argued that educational opportunity costs are irrelevant for purposes of prescribing public policy, of predicting student behavior, or of educational planning. We have not said that the poor would not allocate more time to education if they were subsidized more than they already are or that they should not be subsidized more than they already are. However, we have said that educational opportunity costs have no bearing on either assertion.

We are reminded of a syllogism Professor Friedman has used to illustrate the alleged proof of the superiority of an income tax over an excise tax: "Socrates is a man; Socrates is X; therefore, all men are X."[32] Just as this syllogism is correct when "X" happens to stand for "mortal" but not when it happens to stand for "Greek," so also do existing opportunity-cost calculations lead to the right answer when individual preferences happen to be structured in one way but not when they happen to be structured in another. Such calculations are irrelevant to the purposes for which they are offered and should be regarded as such—lest they prove misleading as well.

NOTES

1. Theodore W. Schultz, "Optimal Investment in College Instruction: Equity and Efficiency," *Journal of Political Economy*, LXXX, No. 3, Part II (May/June, 1972), S10. See also Schultz, *The Economic Value of Education* (New York: Columbia University Press, 1963), p. xi; Schultz, *Investment in Human Capital* (New York: The Free Press, 1971), p. 167; Gary S. Becker, "The Economics of Education," in *The Changing American Economy*, ed. by John R. Coleman (New York: Basic Books, Inc., 1967), p. 203; and Becker, *Human Capital* (New York: National Bureau of Economic Research, 1964), pp. 74–75.

2. Mary Jean Bowman, "The Costing of Human Resource Development," in *The*

Economics of Education, ed. by E. A. G. Robinson and J. E. Vaizey (New York: St. Martins Press, 1966), pp. 432, 422.

3. As offered, for example, by Albert Fishlow, "Levels of Nineteenth-Century American Investment in Education," *Journal of Economic History,* XXVI (December, 1966), 418–36; Theodore W. Schultz, "Capital Formation by Education," *Journal of Political Economy,* LXVIII (December, 1960), 571–83; and Lewis C. Solmon, "Opportunity Costs and Models of Schooling in the Nineteenth Century," *Southern Economic Journal,* XXXVII (July, 1970), 66–83.

4. As assured by the definition $nwt = et + lt$, whereby the price of education time is constant relative to the price of leisure time.

5. We have assumed that $\dfrac{\partial u}{\partial i \partial et} = \dfrac{\partial U}{\partial i \partial lt} = 0$ so that the contours of u, represented in the right-hand graph, will be unaffected by changes in i.

6. Bowman, p. 433.

7. Schultz, *Investment in Human Capital,* pp. 102, 108.

8. We take the expression "earnings opportunity" to be the earnings NM which were realized by the student before he allocated the additional lump of time to education.

9. Jack Wiseman, "Cost-Benefit Analysis in Education," *Southern Economic Journal,* XXXII, No. 1, Part 2 (July, 1965), 7.

10. This distinction is due to James M. Buchanan, *Cost and Choice* (Chicago: Markham Publishing Company, 1969), pp. 44–45.

11. Lewis C. Solmon, "A Note on Equality of Educational Opportunity," *American Economic Review,* LX (September, 1970), 768.

12. *Ibid.,* p. 771.

13. No lump-sum subsidy, however large, would generate the desired expansion if the left-hand expansion path rotated around Z to the horizontal position ZQ, if the right-hand expansion path rotated around I to a position above IH, or if the right-hand expansion path shifted to a vertical position to the left of DH.

14. According to Solmon, "A Note on Equality of Educational Opportunity," p. 768, "adjustments necessitated by a $300 reduction in income for a family earning $3000 probably hurt a youth's ability to benefit from schooling more than does a $600 reduction. . . .in income of a family earning $6000." In that context, we assume that each student contracts his earned income by the same percentage $(LG/CV = LW/CZ)$ in order to achieve the desired expansion of education time.

15. *Ibid.,* p. 768n.

16. Richard A. Musgrave, *The Theory of Public Finance* (New York: McGraw-Hill Book Company, Inc., 1959), pp. 98–108.

17. A seminal exposition is provided by Gary S. Becker, *Human Capital and the Personal Distribution of Income* (Ann Arbor: Institute of Public Administration and Department of Economics, University of Michigan, 1967), pp. 2–12.

18. *Ibid.,* p. 9.

19. Mary Jean Bowman, "Converging Concerns of Economists and Educators," in *Education and the Economics of Human Capital,* ed. by Ronald A. Wykstra (New York: The Free Press, 1971), p. 63.

20. Gary S. Becker, "A Theory of the Allocation of Time," *Economic Journal,* LXXV (September, 1965), 493.

21. "Opportunity Costs and Models of Schooling in the Nineteenth Century," p. 77.

22. Solmon, *ibid.*, concedes as much when he relates a counterargument that shows why demand might rise with income and why "the net effect of income on the demand side is unclear."

23. As suggested by Bowman, "The Costing of Human Resources Development," pp. 434–35.

24. "Optimal Investment in College Instruction," p. S15n.

25. *The Economic Value of Education*, p. 6.

26. Solmon, "A Note on Equality of Educational Opportunity," p. 769.

27. P. 426. See also Schultz, "Optimal Investment in College Instruction," p. S15, and Solmon, "A Note on Equality of Educational Opportunity," p. 769.

28. See Solmon, "A Note on Equality of Educational Opportunity," p. 770. It is interesting that Solmon uses this evidence to *support* his argument that the poor are discriminated against and therefore ought to be subsidized to attend school.

29. *Investment in Human Capital*, p. 168, and "Optimal Investment in College Instruction," pp. S10–S11.

30. "A Theory of the Allocation of Time," p. 493.

31. "Opportunity Costs and Models of Schooling in the Nineteenth Century," p. 75.

32. Milton Friedman, "The 'Welfare' Effects of an Income Tax and an Excise Tax," in *Essays in Positive Economics* (Chicago: University of Chicago Press, 1953), pp. 111–12.

Comments on "On the Irrelevance of Educational Opportunity Costs"

R. D. Auster*

People seldom do anything for one and only one reason. To be sure some motivations are stronger than others, but in general people seem to have many motives for any given action. This must be recognized when dealing with education—or more properly schooling, just as it must with all other human activities. Similarly, if we are to understand equilibrium values in a world where individuals interact with each other, and equilibrium results from the interaction of forces, we will generally need to know how all the participants act and interact, not simply those from one side of the market or another. The pure Human Capital (HC) tradition in the economics of education seems to ignore both these obvious truths in practice. Not surprisingly then, estimates of rates of return to schooling based on this theory may be biased, and policy implications based on these rates of return may be erroneous.

*University of Arizona.

Professors McKnew and Tuerck have nicely articulated one glaring omission of the HC approach. People go to school not only because they desire future income, but also because they derive satisfaction (positive or negative) from the schooling itself. Once this is taken into account, they demonstrate quite clearly that many of the usual comparative statics theorems and policy prescriptions of the HC approach do not hold unless one imposes further restrictions on the nature of the underlying utility functions.

It is important, I think, to recognize that McKnew and Tuerk are not talking about forces of clearly lesser importance than the investment or HC effect. Economists typically refer to the micro decision unit for consumption as "the household." We should recognize then that the child's level of achievement (number of years of school completed) is decided not simply by the child, but by the household and, therefore, that consumption aspects for the household include the parents' consumption of the child's performance.[1] In this broader—yet somewhat traditional—microeconomic theory context, one obtains a simple way of introducing the effects of variations in the parents' income and tastes for knowledge on the child's level of educational attainment, and, observe that these predictions cannot be made by the simple HC model. An even more fully articulated household decision model might be an interesting tack for future research on the schooling process. Models which focus on the Public Choice problems in the household's determination of the level of schooling of its children would appear to me to be particularly promising.

There are many other supply side factors which the HC school essentially ignores in practice. Different levels of schooling are required for entry into different occupations and these have different riskiness in the sense of unemployment experiences, etc. Attitudes towards risk will have an influence on the choice of level of schooling. A considerable literature has grown up in recent years which articulates various other supply side failings of the HC approach, these seem to be significant and McKnew and Tuerk are in that tradition; one only wishes that they had empirically implemented their model. Let us move on, however.

History is not unilinear, it weaves and turns, and often appears to be repeating itself, at least approximately. In the history of thought on any matter, old ideas are rediscovered, and sometimes these are old and incorrect ideas. The classical economists stressed supply, that is relative costs, and neglected demand (tastes) in their theory of relative price. When the HC school gets to the point of empirically implementing the theory, it falls into that classical error. Essentially, the HC theory is a partial theory of the labor supply. When empirically implemented, the rate of return to education is estimated by a regression of the general form

$$\log \text{Earning} = a + c \,(\text{Education}) \tag{1}$$

(where sometimes, however, education is made a vector and different "rates" are estimated for different levels of education). Thus a theory of labor supply is converted to a theory of the distribution of earnings, before being "tested." Now it does seem curious to see what is essentially a theory of the acquisition of human capital, "tested" by being used to predict not levels of schooling, but rather levels of earnings, and one cannot but suspect that independent and dependent variables have been reversed. Leaving this issue aside, however, there are more important criticisms which could, and have, been raised against using estimates of "rates" so obtained for any policy purpose, and against interpreting the quality of the fit of such an equation as evidence for, or against, the HC theory. We now turn to these.

If one is to estimate the rate of return to education, one must take into account forces from the demand side of labor markets as well as supply side forces, and one must take care to see that one has in fact identified the curve one is trying to estimate. As is well known, simply regressing price on quantity does not always give one the supply curve for a product. It would seem that the traditional HC estimation of the rate of return does not adequately take this into account.

The problem is especially serious in the particular institutional context of our times. If attendance at school is compulsory till a certain age, is not all of the variation in the level of school attained up to the maximum achievable in that number of years simply then a function of ability, and if this is so, and more able people are paid more anyway—because they are more productive—then can we identify the rate of return to schooling itself? Various studies using data sources specially suited to attempt such a separation suggest that much of the "return" is in fact a return to ability and other factors,[2] and not schooling.

As with all other prices, wages are determined by both supply and demand side forces in labor markets. The HC equation omits, for example, the potential effect of differences in the relative prices (availability) of other factors of production on the demand for laborers and through that on the wage structure. Yet, Griliches has provided evidence that "skill" or education is more complementary with physical capital than unskilled or "raw labor."[3] As this demand side force has been shown to exist, the implicit assumption of the HC school, that all such forces can be neglected must then be rejected.

Even in a model where a rigorous "labor in efficiency units" existed—in which case the Griliches effect could not exist, the HC approach would lead us to an incorrect estimate of the rate of return to education if marginal revenue product hiring forces were effective, unless the elasticity of substitution at the level of the individual between the qualities of labor associated with schooling (that is, those that vary with it) and those that do not, were either zero, one, or infinity. If this is not the case, then the coefficient the HC school would have us take as an estimate of the rate of return to schooling is biased downward (if we have the law of diminishing returns) and is not the rate of return in any case. This is easy enough to see. Suppose L, the level of labor in efficiency units, is given by a CES defined over the characteristics of the laborer, that is

$$L = B(k_1 X^b + k_2 S(X,E)^b)^{1/b} \qquad (2)$$

where X is a vector of other characteristics of the worker and S is an arbitrary function. Workers in this world are paid the price of a standard unit of labor (P_L) times the amount of labor, L, they supply in one payment period $(P_L \cdot L)$. In this case, earnings (W) will be (approximately)

$$W = k_2^{-\sigma} \left(\frac{\Delta W}{\Delta E} \right)^{\sigma} S \left(\frac{\partial s}{\partial E} \right)^{\sigma} \qquad (3)$$

where

$$\sigma = \frac{1}{1 - b}, \text{ the elasticity of substitution}$$

and $\frac{\Delta W}{\Delta E}$ is a direct estimate of the rate at which wages change when education changes *ceteris paribus*.[4] If we further assume that the elasticity of S with respect to E is constant (say δ) then (3) can be rewritten as

$$\text{Log } W = \alpha + \sigma \log \left(\frac{\Delta W}{\Delta E} \right) + \lambda \text{Log } E \qquad (4)$$

where

$$\alpha = \log k_2 + \log \lambda + \sigma \log \lambda \delta$$

$$\lambda = \delta - \delta \sigma + \sigma$$

which bears a striking similarity to the HC equation *(2)*. Even if the world were exactly like *(4)*, that is, only demand forces were effective, *(2)* could still give one good fit, but would be entirely misleading about the rate of return to E.[5] That such equations do give one a good fit does not provide us with any evidence for the HC theory of the wage structure and therefore cannot be used to provide justification for using estimates of "c" as rates of return to E, unless one can provide some evidence that one has in fact identified *(2)* and not a misspecification of *(4)*. Further, if *(4)* holds, there is a schedule of rates—not one rate of return. Social policy cannot be based on estimates of "c."

In summary then, McKnew and Tuerk provide us with yet more grounds for suspecting that the HC model is entirely inadequate for use in policy applications. Sound estimation and policy requires full models of the markets involved. The problems of simultaneity and multiple causation cannot be wished away.

NOTES

1. Interestingly, in the context of health care we have found that consumption effects dominate investment effects in the demand for hospital care. R. D. Auster and K. K. Ro, "The Demand for Hospital Care by Hospitalized Individuals." Paper presented at the winter '72 Econometric Society Meetings.

2. Taubman and Wales, "Higher Education, Mental Ability and Screening," (*JPE*, Vol. 81, No. 1, Jan/Feb., 1973, pp. 28–55) find ability an important determinant of earnings for this non-compulsory education group. Hansen, Weisbrod and Scanlon, "Schooling and Earnings of Low Achievers," (*AER*, June 1970, pp. 409–18) find these other factors to be important for low achievers. They say "The results presented here demnstrate the misconception of postulating highly significant simple relationships between schooling and earnings, especially for low achievers." One must also remember that disutilities of work also vary and that pure money rates must therefore be adjusted.

3. See Z. Griliches, "Capital-Still Complementarity", *R. E. Stat.*, Vol. LI, No. 4, (Nov. 1969), pp. 465–68.

4. In principle, one could estimate $\frac{\Delta W}{\Delta E}$ by regressing W on E at the level of the individual within categories which held these "other" characteristics (e.g., color, age, sex) constant. When each E is coded as a *separate* dummy variable, the coefficients of that regression across individuals yield unbiased estimates of $\frac{\Delta W}{\Delta E}$.

5. Preliminary estimates of σ indicate it may not in fact be significantly different from zero at conventional levels. These estimates, however, did not use the techniques of fn. 4, but cruder ones to get $\frac{\Delta W}{\Delta E}$ and had a very small sample size. Using the Census's PUS tapes, we hope to be able to eventually report estimates of somewhat greater reliability.

5

Discrimination Based on Education in the Engineering Labor Market

Edmund H. Mantell*

1. Introduction and Objectives

Economists have begun to question the efficiency and equity of the educational system as a mechanism for accumulating capital and determining the distribution of income.[1] This research will focus on a particular form of labor market imperfection which is thought to be induced by the trend towards ever increasing amounts of schooling for larger numbers of people. This market imperfection takes the form of hiring discrimination based on formal education, henceforth called "screening." Screening is defined formally in the following way.[2]

> Screening based on education occurs if, because of lack of formal educational attainment, a person is excluded from an occupation in which he would have a higher marginal product than in that in which he is currently employed.

The screening phenomenon has attracted increasing attention from scholars and educators in recent years. A typical expression of concern is the following:[3]

*Economic Research Division, John Hancock Mutual Life Insurance Company. This paper has been extracted from the author's doctoral dissertation, "The Labor Market for Professional Engineers," submitted to the University of Pennsylvania in 1972. The author would like to express his thanks to Prof. Paul Taubman, supervisor of the dissertation, and Prof. F. Gerard Adams, both of the University of Pennsylvania. The views expressed within the paper are the responsibility of the author alone.

Arbitrarily, on the basis of our own unquestioned faith in schooling, we have decided that the uncredentialed—the unschooled—are unworthy to work on an assembly line or to join pipe, install electric wiring, build houses, read blueprints, program computers, or test chemicals. Although such work may require but a fraction of the potential abilities of any average man with an average schooling, we deny the work to those who have not endured the prescribed number of hours in classrooms to certify for graduation.

It has been alleged that in a number of occupations higher education does not directly contribute to occupational competence, and within these occupations the amount of education is poorly correlated with income.[4] Several social commentators have urged a de-emphasis of "credentialism" and suggested that employers make greater efforts to evaluate applicants as individuals instead of treating them as members of educational classes.

Almost all of the attention which screening has generated has been based on "armchair" empiricism. The objective of this research is to subject the screening hypothesis to a rigorous statistical test within the context of the labor market for professional engineers. The engineering manpower market was thought to be a suitable testing ground for two reasons: (1) there is a substantial amount of *prima facie* evidence to suggest the existence of screening in this labor market[5] and; (2) the equilibrium status of the engineering labor market has been the subject of a lively and continuing controversy for the past twenty years.

2. *Development of a Test of the Screening Hypothesis*[6]

In order to ascertain whether screening has been practiced we will compare the educational distribution of engineering labor in two market scenarios. First we will determine the expected educational distribution of engineers in the absence of any labor market imperfections. The competitive market *ex ante* distribution will then be compared with the *ex post* educational distribution of the engineers in the sample. In a comparison of these two distributions the disparities (if any) will reveal the presence of screening.

The test may be stated more rigorously by considering the postulated mechanism of occupational choice. Suppose that there are N occupation alternatives available to the decisionmaker. Let money earnings in occupation j be denoted by Y_j where Y_j is assumed to be a random variable. Suppose the decisionmaker has complete knowledge of the probability distribution for each $Y_j (j = 1,...,N)$. The person selecting an occupation to enter is presumed to choose that occupation which offers the greatest likelihood of maximum earnings. The decisionmaker must use the information at his disposal to select an occupation such that the probability distribution of earnings in the chosen occupation is preferred to the distribution in any other occupation. Stated another way, the decisionmaker evaluates his earnings expectations in each of the N occupations and selects the occupation in which the probability that earnings shall not be exceeded is maximized.

We can formally express the mechanism of occupational choice as follows: The probability that an individual will prefer to enter occupation j is given by:

(1) $P_j = Pr(Y_j \geq Y_1; Y_j \geq Y_2; \ldots, Y_j \geq Y_{j-1}; Y_j \geq Y_{j+1}; \ldots, Y_j \geq Y_N)$

The randomized decision rule symbolized in *(1)* does not incorporate adjustments for differing attitudes towards risk. It will be assumed that the utility function of the decisionmaker is linear thereby obviating considerations of risk aversion.

In order to obtain an operationally tractable expression for the probability function symbolized in *(1)* we will assume that earnings in each of the N occupations are statistically independent. Let $F_j(\cdot)$ be the cumulative probability distribution of earnings in occupation j and let $\int_j(\cdot)$ be its point density function. Then an operational expression for P_j can be written as:

(2) $P_j = \int_0^\infty f_j(Y) \left(\prod_{i \neq j} F_i(Y) \right) dY$

In the specification of the earnings distribution functions it will be assumed that they are Gaussian. Consequently they can be characterized by only two parameters, the mean and the variance.[7] The mean earnings in occupation j will be denoted by $\bar{Y}_j$ and its associated standard deviation will be denoted by σ_j. Thus $Y_j \sim N(\bar{Y}_j, \sigma_j^2)$.

Suppose $P(E_i)$ represents the probability that a person with education level $E_i(i = 1,...,m)$ prefers to enter the engineering occupation. We may obtain estimates of the probability distribution $\{P(E_i)/i = 1,...,m\}$ by using unbiased estimates of $(\bar{Y}_j, \sigma_j{}^2)$ for each occupation (including engineering). In this context the term "unbiased" means that the parameter estimates must be standardized at the level of education E_i for given levels of innate abilities; on-the-job training (OJT); personality characteristics; and whatever other variables are systematically associated with earnings in each of the occupations. The estimates of the parameter pairs for each of the N occupations are then applied to expression *(3)* to obtain $P(E_i)$:

$$(3) \quad P(E_i) = \int_0^\infty N(\bar{Y},\sigma^2) \left[\frac{N}{\pi} \int_0^Y N(\bar{Y}_j,\ \sigma_j{}^2)\ dY_j \right] dY \quad \text{for } i = 1,...,m$$

where the parameter pair $(\bar{Y},\sigma^2)$ is the standardized mean and variance of earnings in the engineering profession.

We may use the estimates $\{P(E_i)/i = 1,...,m\}$ to derive the *ex ante* competitive educational distribution of engineers. That distribution will be denoted by $\{P_i/i = 1,...,m\}$. Suppose we consider each individual in our sample at the point in time when he has completed his formal education and is contemplating entry into engineering or one of the other N occupations. We denote the number of such individuals at level of education E_i by n_i. In competitive labor markets the expected number of people with education E_i who enter the engineering profession is calculated as $n_iP(E_i)$. The small sample estimator which can be used to estimate $\{P_i\}$ is written as:[8]

$$(4) \quad \bar{P}_i = \frac{1 + n_iP(E_i)}{m + \sum_{i=1}^{m} n_iP(E_i)} \quad i = 1,...,m$$

The same estimator is applied to obtain the *ex post* educational distribution of engineers. In the *ex post* estimation, however, the terms $n_iP(E_i)$ are replaced by the observed number of engineers in the sample with education E_i. By observing the discrepancies (if any) between the *ex ante* and *ex post* distributions at the lower educational levels we can test for the presence of screening.[9]

3. *Implementation of the Test for Screening*

Section 2 indicated that the test for screening entailed the use of standardized estimates of means and variances of the earnings streams all relevant occupations. The standardization requires observations on people with given education, abilities, etc. In general we require observations in an occupation on people with different amounts of education, etc. in order to investigate the relationship between education and earnings in that occupation. This information is contained in the body of data which we shall use to carry out the test. The data consist of longitudinal observations on a cohort of professional engineers as well as cohorts in other occupations. These data were gathered by Thorndike & Hagen and the National Bureau of Economic Research. This body of data will be referred to as the NBER-TH sample.[10]

The standardization may be carried out by estimating the parameters of earnings profiles in each of the N occupations. The earnings profiles are linear (in the parameters) functions of the explanatory variables which are systematically related to earnings in a given occupation. The general specification of the earnings profile is of the form:

$$Y_j(t) = \sum_k b_{jk}X_k + u_j \quad (j = 1,\ldots,N)$$

where $\quad Y_j(t)$ = money earnings in occupation j at age t

$(X_1, X_2, \ldots)$ = determinants of earnings

$(b_{j1}, b_{j2}, \ldots)$ = coefficients unique to occupation j

u = a randomly distributed disturbance term.

The specification of the test for screening assumes that $u_j \sim N(O, \sigma_j^2)$. In addition the specification requires the disturbance terms to be distributed independently.

Regression estimates of the earnings profiles in engineering, and in all other relevant occupations, will partially control for those factors besides education which systematically affect earnings. In other words the essence of the regression is that engineer *A*, who is identical to engineer *B* in all respects except education, would have received the same earnings as *B* if he had only had the same education as *B*. Since many relevant characteristics are unmeasurable (e.g., psychic forms of income), we will be unable to standardize explicitly for them in the estimates. Such characteristics may cause persons with given levels of education and innate ability to select different occupations. Also there may be a purely random element affecting earnings within and between occupations thereby resulting in different occupational choices of persons with given education, ability, etc. All of the omitted variables are subsumed in the disturbance terms.

We proceed to standardize earnings profiles by an application of Factor Analysis to the Vector of 17 intelligence-aptitude test scores for each person in the NBER-TH sample.[11] The objective of this procedure is to "explain" the observable elements in the vector of test scores in terms of a smaller number of unobservable factors. The usefulness of Factor Analysis in most empirical investigations largely depends on the investigator's success in identifying these factors with intuitively observable entities. In our case the intuitive interpretations of the estimated factor loadings are not of primary interest. We employ the technique mainly as a standardizing procedure.

The vectors of individual test scores were normalized to mean zero and standard deviation of one. The estimation of the matrix of factor loadings was then carried out by A. Beaton for the 9,700 persons in the NBER-TH sample. The estimation of factor loadings indicated that the first four orthogonal factors represented over 94 percent of the total variation in the vector of test scores. These will be denoted symbolically by the vector (F_1, F_2, F_3, F_4). The factor F_1 appeared to reflect mathematical aptitude; F_2 — manual dexterity; F_3 — reading comprehension and mechanical skills; F_4 — spatial orientation abilities.[12]

The standardization for psychological characteristics such as ambition, perseverance, and congeniality poses some very difficult problems. Pilot studies experimented with such variables as parental education, religious preference, political attitudes and a variety of "social" attitudes. These variables were used singly and in combination but their explanatory power was negligible. Only one "psychological type" variable proved to be of statistical significance—the information contained in the so-called "Biographical Data Blank" constructed by Thorndike.[13]

> The Biographical Data Blank yielded 112 distinct items of information. These dealt with matters of family background and setting, liking for and success in school subjects, extracurricular activities, hobbies and work experience.

A convex combination of scores contained in the Biographical Data Blank for each engineer (Bio) was used to standardize for variations in "personality effects."

The systematic effects of on-the-job training (OJT) are thought to be of dominating importance in determining earnings within schooling groups. Age, by itself, is not a human capital variable, but the growth of earnings with age is interpretable by the human capital model as a consequence of continued self-investment activities after completion of schooling. Hence to extend the specification of the earnings profile to a more complete function we should introduce age as a conditioning variate. While age is not the same as OJT the latter can be estimated as: $OJT = Age - e - m$, where e is years of formal education and m is length of military service.

Preliminary analyses indicated that the engineers in the NBER-TH sample could be grouped into statistically significant subsamples defined by level of educational attainment. These are defined below:

E_1 No formal education beyond high school[14]

E_2 Some college attendance, degree not awarded

E_3 Undergraduate degree awarded (B.A. or B.S.)

E_4 Some graduate school attendance, graduate degree not awarded

E_5 Graduate degree awarded (M.S. and/or Ph.D.)

Regression estimates of the earnings profile for engineers will be carried out using OLS methods within each of the five educational groups. The engineering profile specification is written as

$$(5) \quad Y(t/E_i) = a_i + b_i(OJT) + \sum_{k=1}^{4} b_{ik}(OJT) \cdot F_j + c_i(OJT) \cdot Bio$$
$$+ \, d_i(OJT)^2 + u_i \quad (i = 1, \ldots, 5)$$

Table 1 displays the OLS estimates of the engineers' earnings profiles together with their test statistics.

The effects of on-the-job training and innate abilities are embodied in the OJT-Factor Score interaction terms. Half of the interaction terms are significant at the .01 level or better. The interaction terms behave erratically across educational classes as is evidenced by changes in sign and in levels of statistical significance. A possible explanation for the seemingly erratic behavior of the OJT-Factor Score coefficients is that engineers with different levels of education gravitate to sub-occupations which require the exercise of selective skills.

The quadratic OJT term is the only explanatory variate which is unambiguously significant in every education class. Theoretical and empirical studies of human capital formation have suggested that the coefficients of the quadratic terms should be negative resulting in an earnings profile shaped like an upside down U. The fact that the quadratic coefficients on Table 1 are positive results from the specification of the dependent earnings variable in current dollars instead of constant dollars which introduces an earnings adjustment for inflation. When OLS regressions were carried out with earnings expressed in constant (1958) dollars the signs of the quadratic terms were all negative.

The test for screening entails the estimation of standardized earnings in all relevant occupations, not just in engineering. We have a consistent set of such profile estimates in the research of Taubman and Wales. Taubman and Wales have utilized the NBER-TH sample to estimate counterpart earnings profiles for the five levels of education in each of seven occupational categories which cover virtually the entire spectrum of labor income. They have analyzed data separately for the occupational categories of: professional; technical; sales; managerial and entrepreneur; white collar; blue collar; and service.[15] In their specification and estimations Taubman and Wales exercised control over systematic varia-

TABLE 1

ESTIMATION OF EARNINGS PROFILES FOR ENGINEERS

(t=Statistics in Parentheses)

Group	Constant	T	$T \cdot F_1$	$T \cdot F_2$	$T \cdot F_3$	$T \cdot F_4$	T·Bio	T^2	R^2	$\hat{\sigma}$	N
E_1	1,347 (4.44)	350 (7.83)	15 (8.87)	-.8 (-.38)	-21 (-7.51)	8 (2.87)	59 (8.20)	6.4 (4.54)	.6968	2,702	1,021
E_2	1,189 (3.07)	277 (5.07)	9 (4.05)	1 (.45)	3 (1.15)	-16 (-5.58)	20 (3.72)	11.6 (6.90)	.6543	3,485	1,499
E_3	-47 (-.08)	407 (6.06)	3 (1.68)	-3 (-1.59)	7 (3.27)	7 (3.15)	3 (.58)	9.6 (5.07)	.4155	5,779	4,938
E_4	1,900 (1.48)	128 (.78)	13 (2.25)	-44 (-7.39)	-90 (-13.01)	105 (11.24)	55 (3.79)	24.1 (5.08)	.6534	5,462	538
E_5	175 (.12)	375 (2.11)	-1 (-.14)	11 (1.65)	10 (1.61)	8 (1.08)	70 (5.36)	15.0 (3.08)	.5886	5,074	769

tions in ability; OJT; some personality characteristics; as well as formal education.

The estimates of the earnings profiles of engineers displayed on Table 1 can be adjusted to reflect differing levels of innate ability, as can the Taubman-Wales estimates. In order to establish comparability both sets were evaluated for persons of average ability (i.e., the average of the NBER-TH sample) after approximately 25 years of OJT.[16] The resulting means and sample standard deviations are displayed on Table 2.

Since there are some occupation-education cells on Table 2 that are empty, it is not possible to obtain estimates of the distributional parameters for these cells. For example, in the NBER-TH sample there are no persons with M.A.'s in the blue collar, white collar, or service occupations. Since it is not possible to determine what the earnings of M.A. holders would be in these occupations, it will be assumed that the advanced graduate degree holders choose only among the other three occupations. The implementation of the test for screening assumes that persons at levels E_1, E_2, E_3 will consider entering any of the eight occupations. Persons with educational levels E_4 *or* E_5 will consider selection only from among the engineering, professional, or managerial occupations.

The earnings data on Table 2 refer only to one point in time. To the extent that lifetime earnings follow widely diverse patterns in different occupations at different age levels, the use of earnings from only one year may be a misleading indicator of lifetime earnings. Taubman and Wales examine the entire NBER-TH sample and conclude that the relative positions of occupations in terms of mean earnings and variance are fairly constant from 1955 to 1969. Thus the selection of a very early year would be likely to entail a bias, because even in the absence of employment screening, in the early years of their working lives many young men at the lower levels of education might choose to enter some occupation other than engineering either because of ignorance of opportunities in engineering, an ill-considered appraisal of the relative attractiveness of the various occupations, a myopic attitude regarding career advancement, or any of a number of other commonplace reasons. As people grow older, it is presumed that they become better in-

TABLE 2

MEAN MONTHLY EARNINGS AND CONDITIONAL STANDARD DEVIATIONS
BY EDUCATION AND OCCUPATION IN 1969

	High School	Some College	Undergrad. Degree	Some Grad. School	M.A. Degree or Higher
Engineering					
mean	1289	1421	1500	1532	1755
std. dev.	225	290	481	455	422
Professional					
mean	960	1260	1412	1315	1493
std. dev.	274	501	674	461	298
Technical					
mean	1220	1285	1370		
std. dev.	577	579	458	na	na
Sales					
mean	1120	1300	1490		
std. dev.	548	614	865	na	na
Blue Collar					
mean	844	882	950		
std. dev.	165	182	244	na	na
Service					
mean	824	882	950		
std. dev.	177	288	244	na	na
	754	785	840		
	127	194	212	na	na
Owner-Mgr.					
mean	1485	1680	1850	1793	1908
std. dev.	907	884	911	1158	1080

na means too few observations to calculate estimates.

formed about the relative attractiveness of the various occupations. Their choice of occupations will thereby reflect a carefully considered judgment of benefits and costs. These judgments may entail voluntary occupational switching or, at the very least, attempted switching. The year 1969 seems an appropriate examination point because it is unlikely that voluntary occupational switching into preferred occupations will not have occurred after 25 years of employment.

An inspection of Table 2 turns up some interesting features of the education-occupation distribution of earnings in the sample. At every level of education the persons in the Owner-Manager category exhibit the highest average monthly earnings invariably coupled with the largest degree of dispersion around that average. This is consistent with the high degree of riskiness usually imputed to the entrepreneurial function. The focus of our concern, however, is the relationship of the earnings distribution in engineering to the earnings distributions in the other occupational categories. It appears that the engineer of average abilities does quite well for himself compared to his expected earnings in any other occupation within a given educational class. Although there is quite a lot of overlap in the earnings distribution within a given educational class, the engineering profession is generally close to the top. The mean earnings in engineering exceed those in every other occupation except Owner-Manager. It can be seen that the spread of engineering earnings is considerably smaller than its closest neighbors —Professional, Technical, and Sales.

An inspection of the last two columns of Table 2 reveals that at the advanced educational levels there is less overlap between the distribution of earnings in engineering and the other professional occupations. A probable consequence of this is that engineering will be more appealing vis-à-vis other professions at levels E_4 and E_5 than it is at the lower educational levels.

Table 3 displays the *ex ante* and *ex post* educational distribution of engineers in the NBER-TH sample. The table has been derived by substituting the conditional means and standard deviations on Table 2 into formula *(3)*. The resulting probabilities are then converted into the *ex ante* distribution by means of the estimator in *(4)*.

TABLE 3

EX ANTE AND *EX POST* DISTRIBUTION OF ENGINEERS IN THE NBER-TH SAMPLE
BY LEVEL OF FORMAL EDUCATION IN 1969

	(1) Actual Number of People	(2) Percentage Desiring Engineering	(3) Expected Number of Engineers	(4) Actual Number of Engineers	(5) Ex Ante Fraction	(6) Ex Post Fraction	Col.(5) −Col.(6)
High School	736	.099	73	31	.176	.065	.111
Some College	852	.135	115	69	.275	.143	.132
Undergrad. Degree	1026	.160	164	278	.390	.571	−.181
Some Grad. School	201	.114	23	44	.056	.094	−.038
M.A. Degree or Higher	575	.074	43	61	.104	.127	−.023
TOTAL	3390	—	418	483	1.000	1.000	—

The *ex post* distribution is obtained by applying *(4)* to the engineers within educational groups in the NBER-TH sample.

Table 3 indicates that in a perfectly competitive market scenario 17.6 percent of the engineering labor force in the sample can be expected to have no formal education beyond high school. In the *ex post* sample distribution the percentage of engineers at that educational level is only 6.5. Thus at the lowest educational level the *ex ante* percentage is more than twice as large as the *ex post* percentage. This finding is regarded as evidence supporting the screening hypothesis. The discrepancy of 11 percentage points indicates that the screening phenomenon accounts for the disproportionately small number of engineers who have no more than a high school education. If screening had not existed (and wage rates had not changed) the number of engineers at E_1 would be much larger than it actually is.

It has been suggested that many persons who have only a year or so of college are likely to develop into competent engineers if they are permitted to acquire experience on the job.[17] The estimated earnings profile for the college-dropout educational class provides some evidence to support this conjecture. However, Table 3 indicates that the *ex ante* fraction of engineers who are college dropouts is twice that of the *ex post* fraction. In this educational class the disparity is more than 13 percentage points. Thus we may infer that employers of engineers have systematically discriminated against college-dropout aspirants for employment. Even though many such people are likely to be productive as engineers, by and large they were not given the opportunity to demonstrate their competence. The evidence on Table 3 implies that screening is practiced at level E_2 as well as E_1.

At the two highest levels of education the expected and actual distributions are nearly coincidental. This indicates that the postulated mechanism of occupational choice does a fairly good job of explaining the educational distribution of engineers at the highest level of education. It is gratifying to observe that the expected fractions of engineers at E_4 and E_5 are not significantly greater than the actual fractions. For if this were the case the power of this test would be called into serious question inasmuch as it is highly implausible that persons with advanced degrees should have been screened out of engineering.

The largest disparity in the comparison of actual with expected educational distributions occurs at the median level of formal-educational attainment. The actual fraction of engineers holding undergraduate degrees substantially exceeds the expected fraction, the difference amounting to 18 percentage points. This difference may be explained by recourse to two psychological type phenomena—a taste for risk combined with the status (prestige) appeal of the engineering profession. *A priori* considerations suggest that these two non-pecuniary sources of income are likely to be operational at least at the margin. Since we have not been able to exercise any control for them they may have combined to produce the observed discrepancy at level E_3.

We have shown that the expected distribution would not be the actual distribution that would prevail in the long run under conditions of free entry. That is, if all entry barriers were removed there would be some changes in the educational distribution of engineers. In a properly functioning market these changes would necessarily result in wage adjustments until the market had again equilibrated at an educational distribution different from that prevailing in the screened market. The expected distribution displayed in Table 3 represents the distribution that would exist if the actual wage structure was also the equilibrium wage structure.

4. *Concluding Remarks*

The major inference of this research is that education-based employment discrimination exists in the labor market for engineers. This labor market imperfection is at least partially responsible for the large disparities observable between the earnings of engineers and their educational counterparts in other occupations (at the lower levels of education).

Some of the policy implications of the screening hypothesis are likely to be uncongenial to those who regard education as a panacea for the ills of society. The National Defense Education Act grants, the National Science Foundation grants, and governmentally subsidized loans have the effect of increasing the supply of engineers (and others) with more advanced levels of higher education. It has been argued that an increase in the general level of education of engineers, *ceteris paribus*, will induce a concomitant elevation of the screening level.[18] To the extent that this elevation response occurs, governmental subsidies to higher education may be counterproductive.

If it is thought proper for the government to assume a role in ameliorating the imperfections which exist in markets for highly trained manpower, then the screening phenomenon appears to be a suitable candidate for governmental attention. Policy makers should take care, however, to attack screening on the grounds of its rationale rather than by providing more education for everyone in the attempt to beat the screen.

NOTES

1. For extensive discussions of many of the issues see the recent series of papers collected in "Investment in Education: The Equity Efficiency Quandary." T. W. Schultz, (ed.), *Journal of Political Economy*, Vol. 80, No. 3, Part II (May/June 1972).

2. The definition is a paraphrase of one devised by Paul Taubman and Terence Wales in *Education as a Screening Device* (unpub. manuscript, March 1970) Dept. of Economics, University of Pennsylvania.

3. James W. Kuhn, "Would Horatio Alger Need a Degree?" *Saturday Review* (December 19, 1970), p. 66. Cf. the comments by the president of Johns Hopkins University Lincoln Garden, "Perhaps Everybody Should Not Go to College," *The Washington Sunday Star* (March 29, 1970), p. D-3. A strong expression of concern is found in a paper given before the American Orthopsychiatric Association in 1967 reprinted in *The Public Interest*, No. 9, (Fall, 1967) p. 127. See also Daniel E. Diamond and Hrach Bedrosian, "Job Performance and the New Credentialism," *California Management Review*, Vol. XIV, No. 4, (Summer, 1972).

4. Dael Wolfle, "Overeducation," *Science*, Vol. CLXVIII, No. 3929 (April 17, 1970), p. 319.

5. Presumptive evidence is contained in Ivar Berg, *Education and Jobs: The Great Training Robbery* (Praeger, N.Y.) 1970, pp. 94–101.

6. The general form of the test for screening was devised by Taubman and Wales, *op. cit.* The test to be applied in this paper is based on their procedure.

7. The mean-variance requirement is a simplifying expedient. We could use a more general specification but at a considerably greater cost in terms of the difficulty of unbiased estimation. This point wilt be clarified in the following discussions.

8. For detailed discussion of the motivation and advantages of using this estimator see I. J. Good, *The Estimation of Probabilities*, Research Monograph No. 30, the M.I.T. Press, 1965, pp. 23–25.

9. The differences between the expected distribution and the actual distribution will reflect *any* market barriers to entry or any systematic deviations from the behavioral assumption of money earnings maximization. If there exist market imperfections other than screening which are systematically associated with formal education, then such imperfections would manifest themselves in the *ex post* distribution but may not be controlled for in the expected distribution.

10. A description of the NBER-TH sample is given by John C. Hause in "Earnings Profile: Ability and Schooling," *Journal of Political Economy*, Vol. 80, No. 3, Part II (May/June 1972). A much more thorough description is given by Robert L. Thorndike and Elizabeth Hagen in *Ten Thousand Careers* (New York: Wiley & Sons) 1959. The cohort of engineers is analyzed extensively in the *Dissertation, op. cit.*, Chap. 3 and Appendix A.

11. A very detailed discussion of the interpretation and statistical usefulness of the test scores is given by Thorndike, *op. cit.*, pp. 55–76.

12. A complete numerical table of the factor loading coefficients is contained in the *Dissertation, op. cit.*, p. 118.

13. Thorndike, *op. cit.*, p. 66.

14. Engineers who received vocational school training after completing high school are included in group E_1. They constitute about 9 percent of the group.

15. These categories were chosen by Taubman and Wales in order to obtain a sufficient number of observations while maintaining homogeneity with respect to average earnings levels. Moreover, the variance of the unexplained residual is approximately constant for the sub-occupations in a group, but the variances differ between occupations.

16. As an estimate of the variance of earnings for an average individual with education E_i we use the conditional variance based on the vector of deviations e = $Y(t/E_i) - Y(t/E_i)$ where $Y(t/E_i)$ is the conditional expectation of earnings resulting from OLS estimates of the earnings profile. The assumption that this variance is the same for non-engineers as for engineers, when estimating what non-engineers would earn if they had become engineers, seems reasonable since the profile estimates purport to control for systematic variations in the determinants of earnings.

17. Cf. the Comments by Joseph D. Mooney, "An Analysis of Unemployment Among Professional Engineers and Scientists," *Industrial and Labor Relations Review*, Vol. XIX, No. 4, (July 1966), pp. 517–28.

18. This hypothesis is discussed in the *Dissertation, op. cit.*, pp. 6–16.

Comments on "*Discrimination Based on
Education in The Engineering Labor Market*"

Malcolm Galatin*

In order to determine the extent of screening in a labor market, Mantell sets out to compare the educational distribution in the occupation if no screening occurs, the ex-ante distribution, with the actual, ex-post, distribution. Discrepancies between the two distributions will then be indicative of the presence of screening.

Thus the results of the paper depend crucially on the way in which the ex-ante distribution is calculated. I believe that the procedure used to estimate the ex-ante distribution is misconceived, which casts doubt on the validity of the empirical results of the paper.

To estimate the ex-ante distribution, which Mantell believes to be the distribution under competitive conditions, a model of occupational choice is constructed based on work by Taubman and Wales. An individual is assumed to know the distributions of income $f_j(Y), j = 1, \ldots, N$, in the N occupations and "selects the occupation in which the probability that earnings shall not be exceeded is maximized." This probability is (Mantell's equation (2))

$$P_j = \int_0^\infty f_j(Y) \left(\prod_{i \neq j} F_i(Y) \right) dY$$

where $F_j(Y)$ is the cumulative distribution function of income in the i'th occupation.

To proceed to a calculation of the ex-ante distribution, the P_j are also interpreted as "the probability that an individual will prefer to enter occupation j." Then the P_j are multiplied by the number of individuals classified by education etc., to obtain the ex-ante distribution in the population. This distribution itself is calculated by the small sample estimator, Mantell's equation *(4)*.

However, it is incorrect to interpret the P_j as probabilities of movement into the j 'th occupation. Although these P_j are prob-

*Associate Professor of Economics, City College of the City University of New York.

abilities, the probability that the distribution of income in occupation j in some sense dominates the income distributions in the other occupations, they can only be interpreted as a utility indicator for *ranking* the income distributions in the occupations. The individual calculates the P_j and *chooses* that occupation which has the highest value of P_j. How else is the first quote above to be interpreted? Thus there is no random mechanism for occupational choice in the paper, for the P_j cannot be interpreted as the probability of moving into the N occupations. Thus the whole procedure for calculating the ex-ante distribution is incorrect.

If we assume that Mantell's basic approach, a comparison of the ex-ante competitive distribution with the ex-post distribution, is a valid method, what is required is a much better model for estimating the ex-ante distribution in the absence of screening. Further work in this area must concentrate on the specification of this model.

6

Income Inequality and Subsidizing Higher Education

George M. Vredeveld*

INTRODUCTION

There has been a long tradition of subsidizing higher education in the United States. While educators agree that subsidizing education increases the quantity of education consumed, there still is considerable disagreement about the income redistributive effects of subsidies. There are those who believe that to abolish tuition and fees, or at least significantly lower them, will benefit the poor by removing financial barriers to higher education. On the other side stand those who agree with Henry George that the taxes of the poor are used "to educate rich men's sons."

Two related studies have considered this problem. Hansen and Weisbrod [7] estimated the distributional effects of subsidies by comparing the size of the subsidies received by students attending each of California's three types (Junior Colleges, State Colleges, and the University of California) of public institutions of higher education, the average income of the families of students attending each type of school, and the average tax burden borne by these families. Hansen and Weisbrod found that the distribution of net

*Assistant Professor, University of Missouri-Columbia. This paper is based on my Ph.D. dissertation (Indiana University). I wish to thank the members of my dissertation committee, Drs. George M. von Furstenberg, Herbert J. Kiesling, Richard L. Pfister, and Ernst W. Stromsdorfer, for their assistance in this study as well as Gerald Auten and David W. Stevens for their helpful comments on this paper. I also wish to acknowledge the financial support provided by the Institute for Applied Urban Economics at Indiana University.

subsidies (i.e., total subsidies less tax burdens) is regressive in the sense that the size of the net subsidy received and the average income of persons receiving that subsidy are positively correlated. Joseph Pechman [16] used Hansen and Weisbrod's data and classified beneficiaries by income class rather than by type of institution attended. Accordingly, Pechman showed that the incidence of California's system of subsidizing higher education is progressive in the sense that for low income classes net subsidies are positive but for high income classes they are negative.

The second study, by Douglas M. Windham [21], centered on subsidies to higher education in Florida. His classification scheme was similar to Pechman's and the one used in this study. Windham found that subsidizing higher education in Florida creates a distributional effect from low income groups to high income groups.

This paper also considers the relative income effects of subsidizing higher education. Its results support the argument that state subsidies to public higher education create a flow of wealth from low income to high income classes.

Higher education, which generally is defined to include all formal schooling beyond the high school level, produces a bundle of goods which can be classified into four categories:

(1) liberal, preprofessional and professional education
(2) fundamental research and preservation of knowledge
(3) applied research
(4) extension and public service

This study's analysis of higher education is limited to (1) the process of educating the undergraduate student which, to a large extent, consists of liberal and preprofessional education, and (2) the distributional impact of the state of Indiana's financial support of its public institutions of higher education.

After the analytical model is defined, this paper will: (1) describe the methods of quantifying educational subsidies and of distributing the benefits of these subsidies by income class, (2) derive the cost incidence of subsidizing education, and (3) estimate the distributional impact of subsidizing higher education by comparing the costs and benefits which accrue to each income class. An appendix is included for those interested in a more detailed account of computations concerning cost incidence and the size of subsidies and benefits.

THE MODEL

In order to measure the redistributive impact of subsidizing education, conceive of an economy in which each individual owns a collection of assets (including the capitalized value of his labor).[1] A government in this economy initially diverts resources from the private sector in order to subsidize education. At time t the government eliminates its subsidy to higher education and simultaneously reduces taxes by an equivalent amount. When adjustments have had a time to work themselves out at a time $t + 1$, each individual will have a new "economic position" relative to other individuals.[2] This change in his "economic position" is brought on by two factors: (a) the decrease in the benefits of an education-subsidy program, and (b) the decrease in taxes.

The income-redistributive effects of aid to public higher education will be estimated using the following procedure:

(1) divide the population of Indiana into income classes
(2) determine the gross benefits which each income class receives from a subsidy to education
(3) determine the incidence of costs by finding the tax share of subsidizing education borne by each income class
(4) find (2) minus (3) for each income class to obtain the direction and magnitude of the income redistributive effects for the respective classes

BENEFITS OF EDUCATIONAL SUBSIDIES

Measurements of Subsidies

Subsidies are defined as that portion of the cost of educating a student which is borne by the state. They are quantified by subtracting from the full cost of educating the student the sum of the costs borne by students, non-state governmental institutions, and other individuals. To isolate the cost of educating a student from the full costs of an institution of higher education, total institutional costs should be allocated among and within the four educational output categories described above. One's success in doing this depends on the extent to which he is able to separate and allocate joint costs. According to traditional theory, joint costs can be attributed to individual products if they are produced in variable proportions. But this theory is based on the usual competitive market assumptions, and these assumptions do not hold in the markets for the products of education.[3]

These difficulties preclude the use of traditional theoretical methods in estimating costs and one is forced to be somewhat arbitrary in isolating the costs of educating the student from the total budget of the school. This arbitrariness notwithstanding, it seems that the resulting estimate of full cost will be closer to the true cost of educating a student than an estimate in which no distinction is made between the different products of the university.

Ideally, the cost of educating a student should be viewed as the value of what the resources used in education could have produced, in their next best alternative use. This opportunity cost concept is not limited to overt expenses or to money transactions which take place as a result of producing education, but includes anything the bearer of the cost must give up when education is produced. In this study the measurement of costs is restricted to marketable or potentially marketable transactions. In those cases where there are no actual money outlays, costs will be measured by the estimated value of the resources in their next best marketable use.[4]

The total cost of educating a student is grouped into five categories: instructional costs; capital costs; books and supplies; room, board and transportation; and foregone earnings. Instructional costs are calculated from the financial reports of the schools. These costs are limited to those incurred for "education of the student," and special categories such as public extension and organized research are not included in the calculations. As proxies for capital costs, the estimated annual rents of the schools' capital are used. All expenses incurred for books and supplies are included, but only the portion of room, board, and transportation expenses which exceed the cost of those services if the student were not to attend school are computed as educational costs. Foregone earnings are based on the average value of time devoted to educational purposes.

After the full cost of education is calculated, the portion of the cost borne by the state must be determined. The largest share of the state-borne costs is received by the student in the form of a "basic subsidy." This subsidy, which is assumed to accrue in equal amounts to all students attending the same school, is equal to full cost less non-state grants received by the institution for educational purposes less standard student costs.[5] Total "basic subsidies" received by each income class are obtained by multiplying the per student subsidy received at each school times the number of students attending that school in each particular income class.

In addition to this "basic subsidy" there are other state-supported programs of financial aid and subsidy which are directed toward specific groups of students.[6] The total value of these subsidies is distributed according to the income class of the recipients of these awards.[7]

A third type of aid given by the state is more indirect than the above subsidies. The Federal Internal Revenue Service (IRS) allows the parents of college students to claim their children as dependents regardless of the student's income so long as the parent contributes at least fifty per cent of the student's support cost. According to Indiana tax laws, a family meeting the federal government's requirements for the dependency allowance may claim the student as a dependent under Indiana's tax laws. In this sense the student's family receives a subsidy from the state. This subsidy is distributed according to the estimated income class of the families who qualify for this exemption.

Measurement of Benefits

In order to measure the benefits of educational subsidies it is important to distinguish between the money cost of the subsidy and the benefits received from the subsidy. Since state support of higher education is given in the form of a tied subsidy, the costs and the benefits of a subsidy in most cases will not be equal. The extent to which these two values differ is illustrated in Figure *1* where the horizontal axis represents the quantity of public higher education and the vertical axis the quantities of all other goods.[8] Given that the price of all other goods (which is assumed to remain

Figure 1
The Inefficiencies of Tied Subsidies

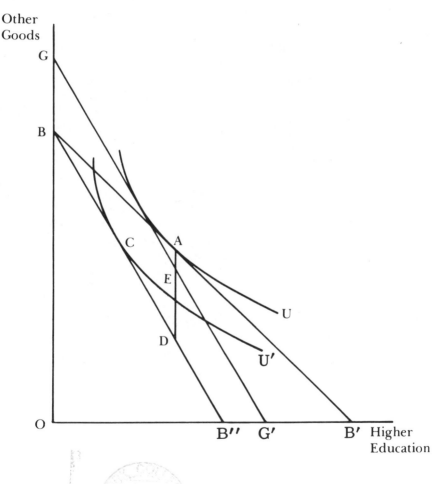

constant) and the subsidized price of education are both unity, a representative individual maximizes his utility at A along his budget line BB'. If the subsidy to education is removed such that the new budget line is BB'', the individual maximizes utility at C. Assuming that there is equal efficiency in the production of education and all other goods, the money cost of the removed subsidy is AD, but the value which the individual places on the subsidy is the compensation needed to get him back to the utility curve U (shown in Figure 1 as DE). The value of the subsidy is less that the money cost of the subsidy (DA) and therefore AE has been "wasted."

The size of the benefit from subsidizing higher education, the relative positions of A and C, and the efficiency of a subsidy depend on the form of the utility function.[9] Although there is a lack of agreement on the exact shape of the utility function, there is basic agreement concerning some of the properties (for example, negative slope and convexity from below) it should exhibit. The utility function used must possess these properties and must also imply price and income elasticities which are consistent with the elasticities of higher education.

The Constant Elasticity of Substitution (CES) class of utility functions is one which satisfies these conditions. It implies a unitary income elasticity of demand but allows the use of a number of price elasticities. The general form of the function is $U = [DX_1^{-p} + (1-D)X_2^{-p}]^{-1/p}$ where D is a distribution parameter and p is a substitution parameter.[10]

The accuracy of using the CES function to estimate the relative efficiencies of educational subsidies depends on the extent to which the value of the parameters used and the unitary income elasticity implication coincide with reality.

The measurement of price elasticities is complicated by the fact that educational products are purchased as part of a larger bundle of educational outputs, some of which are not priced. This purchase of a bundle of priced and unpriced goods rather than individually purchased goods can confuse the measurement of demand elasticities since it is difficult to determine whether the individual is responding to change in the price of a good or to the quality and/or quantity of an unpriced good. Furthermore, if there are quantity constraints to the purchase of education, income and price elasticities will be understated.[11]

Because of these difficulties, the following sets of price elasticities are used to measure the benefits of an educational subsidy:

(1) a price elasticity of demand of −.44 for all income groups——to be consistent with Campbell and Siegel's [5] estimate

(2) a price elasticity of −.8—to adjust for quantity or ability constraints which may exist

(3) price elasticities calculated by Hoenack [10] which make it possible to distinguish by income class They are: −.68 for the income class $0–7,499; −.59 for the income class $7,500–11,999; −.55 for the income class $12,000–14,999; and −.48 for the income class of $15,000 and above.

There have been several estimates of the income elasticity of demand for higher education. Galper and Dunn [6] calculated the income elasticity of demand for college education to be +.69. Oostheimer [15] used national cross section data in calculating an income elasticity of +.79. Campbell and Siegel [5] calculated an income elasticity of +1.2 using time series data from 1919 to 1964. According to Census Bureau data [19], the proportion of income spent on higher education is an approximately constant percentage for all income classes (except the lowest and highest extremes), implying income elasticity near unity.[12] Although there remains a lack of agreement on the magnitude of the income elasticity of demand for higher education, no "returns-to-scale" adjustments are made and therefore the income elasticity has been assumed to be unity.

To estimate the distribution parameter the amount of money spent on education is calculated as a percentage of the total income of units "eligible" to purchase education. An "eligible unit" is defined as a family or other decision unit which has at least one member under 24 years of age who has been or will be graduated from high school.[13]

Table *1* summarizes the distribution of per capita subsidies and their benefits. Column *3* shows per capita subsidies received by income class. Columns 4–6 illustrate the effects of using the *CES*

TABLE 1

Distribution of Per Capita
Educational Subsidies by Income Class
1969-70[1]

(1) Gross Income Class	(2) Number of Families and Unrelated Individuals[2]	(3) Per Capita Subsidies[3]	(4) Per Capita Benefits Using −.44 as Price Elasticity[4]	(5) Per Capita Benefits Using −.8 as Price Elasticity[4]	(6) Per Capita Benefits Using Varying Price Elasticities[4]
$ 0- 2,999	355,220	7.94 (7.60)	6.33 (6.05)	5.80 (5.55)	5.93 (5.67)
3,000- 5,999	271,072	24.35 (22.92)	18.47 (17.39)	16.65 (15.67)	17.19 (16.18)
6,000- 7,499	164,118	38.96 (37.17)	28.76 (23.89)	25.53 (21.22)	26.73 (22.19)
7,500- 8,999	166,418	40.66 (38.10)	31.32 (29.35)	28.56 (26.76)	30.18 (28.28)
9,000-11,999	315,686	62.60 (61.47)	45.72 (44.90)	40.03 (39.31)	43.55 (42.77)
12,000-14,999	212,551	89.03 (85.71)	65.27 (62.83)	54.88 (52.83)	63.38 (61.01)
15,000-19,999	202,289	88.30 (81.48)	64.88 (59.87)	57.47 (53.04)	64.88 (59.87)
20,000+	60,096	357.88 (325.72)	265.65 (241.79)	236.02 (214.82)	264.04 (240.32)

[1] Parenthesized figures refer to subsidy estimates when no research costs are attributed to students.
[2] Taken from U.S. Bureau of the Census [18].
[3] This is the ratio of total subsidies and number of families and unrelated undividuals (Column 2).
[4] Columns 4-6 are found by dividing estimated benefits of subsidies by the number of families and unrelated individuals (Column 2 of this Table).

utility function to reduce the subsidies to cash-equivalent grants. These results show that, except for the $15,000–19,999 income group, there is a positive correlation between income and size of subsidy—that is, the magnitude of per capita subsidies increases with each successively higher income class.

COSTS OF SUBSIDIZING EDUCATION

Tax Incidence Theory

The incidence of the costs of subsidizing higher education depends directly on which taxes are used to finance the subsidy, who bears the burden of those taxes, and the extent to which particular taxes are reduced (increased) when subsidies are reduced (increased).

In a competitive economy the burden of all general taxes can be shown to be proportional to an individual's share of total income. However, the analysis of partial or discriminatory taxes is more complex. In considering the incidence of partial taxes, three basic effects must be analyzed: (a) the demand effect, (b) the output (factor-intensity) effect, and (c) the factor-substitution effect.[14]

The demand effect depends on the individual's consumption patterns. From the viewpoint of the demand effect alone, a partial excise tax in industry X will be more burdensome to individual A than to individual B if A buys primarily good X and B buys primarily good Y.

The output effect depends on relative factor-intensities of the two industries and the elasticity of factor substitution in X and Y. A tax in industry X will cause the price of X to increase and the quantity demanded to decrease. If there are two factors (m and n) and the production of X is m-intensive relative to Y, the price of m will decrease since the factors not used in the production of X cannot be fully absorbed in industry Y at the pre-tax price of m. Thus, considering only the output effect, a tax imposed in an industry will cause the relative price of the factor used most intensively in that industry to fall, and the relative price will fall to a greater extent the less the elasticity of factor substitution in the industries.[15]

Factor-substitution effects occur only when a partial factor tax is imposed in one of the two sectors. Under perfect competition a factor will receive the same after-tax payment in the production of X as it will in the production of Y. If a tax is imposed on factor m in the X industry the relative price of m (including the tax) must increase in that industry, causing a substitution of factor n for m. Consequently, m will be more plentiful in the untaxed industry and its after-tax payment will fall.

To estimate a state's tax incidence, some aspects of inter-regional incidence must be considered. In this case, incidence depends on the three effects discussed above as well as the mobility of the factors of production. For example, conceive of a state's economy in which one factor (e.g., capital) is mobile but another factor (e.g., labor) is not mobile. With the imposition of a tax there will be an increase in prices, a reduction in output, and capital will move to other regions.[16] The immobile factor will bear a major burden of the tax since, unless the returns to labor or other immobile factors decrease, investment in the state will be less profitable than in other states.

Also, consider the case where all factors are immobile. A commodity tax will be borne by the factors of production if output prices do not change. If, because of strong labor unions, administered prices, or other practices inconsistent with perfect markets, the tax is shifted forward to prices, the incidence of the tax will depend on consumption patterns.

Sources of Revenue for Education Subsidies

An accurate measurement of the cost incidence also entails knowledge of which taxes will be reduced and the magnitude of their reduction. Since no taxes are clearly earmarked for subsidizing higher education, it is difficult to state unequivocally which taxes will be affected by a reduction in educational subsidies. However, certain groups of taxes are eliminated as candidates for reduction.

The first group includes those taxes whose revenues are earmarked for purposes other than higher education. Since the revenue of these taxes is not used to support higher education, changes in the level of subsidies to higher education should have little effect on these taxes.[17]

A second group includes the taxes whose revenues are used to finance the output of local governmental goods and services. To assume that local taxes will not vary with a change in expenditures at the state level implies that there is no interaction between the provision and finance of state and local goods. Although this implication is not consistent with reality, one cannot be certain of the direction or the magnitude of a change in municipal tax burdens due to a variation in the level of subsidizing higher education.[18] Because of these difficulties and the strong possibility that municipal taxes would be affected only to a small degree with a change in the level of subsidizing education, local tax burdens are not taken explicitly into account in the calculations of cost incidence.

Measuring Cost Incidence in Indiana

In order to estimate the reduction in tax burdens due to the elimination of the education subsidy, it is assumed that the percentage decrease in each income group's taxes (except those previously excluded) is equal to the proportion of the government's total expenditures spent on higher education subsidies.[19]

Furthermore, the following simplifying assumptions about Indiana's economy will be made: (a) the total supply of factors in the nation as a whole is inelastic, (b) on average, before-tax-factor-intensity in Indiana firms is the same as the factor-intensity for the nation as a whole, (c) the mobility of captial is greater than the mobility of labor, and land is perfectly immobile. Assumption *a* is included in order to limit the analysis to a reasonably short time frame (five years, for example). It implies that the effects of the tax are not merely temporary adjustments along the path back to the original pre-tax equilibrium factor price ratios. Because of assumption *b*, the imposition of a commodity tax will create no pressures for relative factor prices to change as a result of relative factor intensities. The implication of assumption *c* is that although the tax will not affect the net return to capital to a great extent, it will affect the net return to labor and land. After the imposition of the tax, *b* will no longer hold since industry will become more labor-intensive because of labor's relative immobility.

Based on these assumptions, tax burdens are distributed among income classes. The results of this distribution are shown below in

Table 2. As in the case of benefits there is a positive correlation between the cost incidence of subsidizing education and income class.

TABLE 2

Distribution of Per Capita Costs
by Income Class
1969-70[1]

Gross Income Class	$0-2,999	3,000-5,999	6,000-7.499	7.500-8,999	9,000-11,999	12,000-14.999	15,000-19,999	20,000 and above
Per Capita Costs	7.27 (6.81)	28.76 (26.96)	40.13 (37.62)	56.19 (52.67)	61.06 (57.24)	79.57 (74.59)	87.80 (82.30)	338.98 (317.74)

[1] Parenthesized figures refer to cost estimates when no research costs were attributed to students.

NET INCIDENCE OF SUBSIDIZING EDUCATION

Assuming that all subsidies are removed and taxes are reduced by the cost of the subsidies, the difference between the benefits received from the subsidies and the tax savings of removing the subsidies is an estimate of the net benefits each income class derives from the subsidization of higher education. These results are calculated by subtracting, for each income class, the costs of the subsidies (Table 2) from the per capita educational subsidies and benefits presented in Table 1. Table 3 shows the per capita gains or losses of subsidizing education for each income class. From Column 2 it can be seen that when the magnitude of subsidies received is compared with the cost of the subsidy, three income groups (those included in the $3,000–8,999 range) suffer a negative income redistributive effect, most of which is borne by the $7,500–8,999 group. For all other income classes the magnitude of subsidies received is greater than the cost of these subsidies. Except for the lowest income class, all of these groups have a mean income above the mean

TABLE 3

Per Capita Net Incidence
of Subsidizing Education
by Income Class
1969-70[1]

(1) Gross Income Class	(2) Net Incidence (Subsidies less Costs)[2]	(3) Net Incidence Using -.44 as Price Elasticity[2]	(4) Net Incidence Using -.8 as Price Elasticity[2]	(5) Net Incidence Using Varying Price Elasticities[2][3]
$ 0-2,999	+.67 (+.79)	-.94 (-.76)	-1.47 (-1.26)	-1.34 (-1.14)
3,000- 5,999	-4.41 (-4.04)	-10.29 (-9.57)	-12.11 (-11.29)	-11.57 (-10.78)
6,000- 7,499	-1.17 (-.45)	-11.37 (-13.73)	-14.60 (-16.40)	-13.40 (-15.43)
7,500- 8,999	-15.53 (-14.57)	-24.87 (-23.32)	-27.63 (-25.91)	-26.01 (-24.39)
9,000-11,999	+1.54 (+4.23)	-15.34 (-12.34)	-21.03 (-17.93)	-17.51 (-14.27)
12,000-14,999	+9.46 (+11.12)	-14.30 (-11.26)	-24.69 (-21.76)	-16.19 (-13.58)
15,000-19,999	+.50 +.82	-22.92 (-22.43)	-30.33 (-29.26)	-22.92 (-22.43)
20,000+	+18.90 (+7.98)	-73.33 (-75.95)	-102.96 (-102.92)	-74.94 (-77.42)

[1] Parenthesized figures refer to subsidy estimates when no research costs were attributed to students.
[2] Net incidence in columns 2, 3, 4, and 5 are found by subtracting per capita costs of subsidies (Table 2) from per capita subsidies and per capita benefits (Columns 3, 4, 5, and 6 respectively in Table 1).

income of the State.[20] When costs of subsidizing education are compared with the *benefits* of subsidies, no income group realizes positive net benefits (see Columns 3–5). These results indicate that the inefficiencies of tied subsidies to higher education are large enough to reduce the benefits of subsidies to less than the costs of subsidies, even for those groups who appeared to be net beneficiaries in Column 2. For the three income classes which showed a net negative effect in Column 2, the inefficiencies of tied subsidies exacerbates this effect.

Table 4 shows the percentage distribution of the costs and benefits of subsidizing higher education. Since the total costs of subsidies equal total subsidies, one can compare the simple transfer effect of subsidizing education. If the percentage figure in Column 3 is greater than the respective figure in Column 2, the subsidies received by that income class are greater than the cost of the subsidies borne by that group. Since benefits of subsidies are less than the costs of subsidies, a simple comparison of percentages in Columns 4–6 with the corresponding figure in Column 2 does not give a clear indication of income redistribution. In the respect that these distributions of benefits illustrate each income group's share of benefits *vis-à-vis* its share of costs, they are informative.

These results sharply contradict those who argue for low tuition charges as a means to help the poor. Although the poor pay a relatively small percentage of the cost of state assistance programs, they receive an even smaller percentage of the benefits. Low tuition policies, therefore, will help a few members of low income classes to a considerable extent, but the vast majority of the poor will incur increased tax burdens without realizing the benefits.

It should be emphasized that these results are not presented as an appeal or argument for more or less financial support to higher education. The study seeks only to identify the direction and magnitude of the redistributive effects of subsidies to higher education. If the resulting transfer of wealth is contrary to the objectives of public support of higher education, some different method of educational finance should be inaugurated.

TABLE 4

Percentage Distribution of
Costs and Benefits
by Income Class
1969-70[1]

(1) Gross Income Class	(2) Cost of Subsidies	(3) Total Subsidies	(4) Benefits Using −.44 as Price Elasticity	(5) Benefits Using −.8 as Price Elasticity	(6) Benefits Using Varying Price Elasticities
$ 0- 2,999	.0257	.0280 (.0286)	.0301 (.0308)	.0314 (.0321)	.0278 (.0311)
3,000- 5,999	.0775	.0656 (.0659)	.0671 (.0675)	.0688 (.0691)	.0644 (.0647)
6,000- 7,499	.0654	.0635 (.0647)	.0633 (.0561)	.0638 (.0567)	.0606 (.0537)
7,500- 8,999	.0929	.0672 (.0672)	.0699 (.0699)	.0724 (.0725)	.0694 (.0694)
9,000-11,999	.1915	.1964 (.1983)	.1935 (.2029)	.1926 (.2020)	.1899 (.1992)
12,000-14,999	.1681	.1880 (.1931)	.1860 (.1884)	.1777 (.1828)	.1861 (.1913)
15,000-19,999	.1765	.1775 (.1747)	.1760 (.1734)	.1772 (.1746)	.1813 (.1787)
20,000+	.2024	.2137 (.2075)	.2140 (.2081)	.2161 (.2101)	.2192 (.2131)
Total	1.0000	1.0000	1.0000	1.0000	1.0000

[1] Parenthesized figures refer to subsidy estimates when no research costs were attributed to students. Column 2 is based on cost data presented in Table 2. Columns 4-6 show the percentage distribution of subsidies and benefits presented in Table 3.

A Note of Caution

There have been some challenges to this study's method of calculating the redistributive effects of expenditure programs. Joseph Pechman [16], for example, has stated that in analyzing the redistributive effects of an educational subsidy program the *future* distribution of college-educated individuals by income class should be considered. He argues that there are two types of wealth transfer. The first is a transfer from existing groups, who pay more for the educational bill than they receive, to other contemporary groups whose subsidies are greater than their share of costs. The second transfer of wealth operates in the direction of those income classes which pay the education bill to the future income classes of the students who receive the subsidies to education.

The difficulty, of course, is to predict the future income classes of students who receive subsidies to education. For example, Christopher Jencks and his colleagues [11] argue that knowledge of a person's family's socio-economic status, his scores on tests of cognitive skills, and his educational attainment are not very helpful in predicting the individual's future income.[21] Without reliable predictors of income it is difficult to measure the type of distributional impact called for by Pechman.

Another challenge to this study's methodology may be based on its ommission of a calculation of external benefits of higher education. Although there may be external benefits, it is difficult to measure them and even more difficult to identify their recipients. However, it is unlikely that the presence of external benefits changes the direction of income redistribution resulting from a subsidy program. For this change to occur, the magnitude of external benefits must be large and a major proportion of these benefits must be received by the poor. Presently, there is no evidence that either of these conditions exist.

NOTES

1. Basically there are two ways in which subsidies to higher education will affect the distribution of income. The first is by altering the market forces which determine income. The second is by means of governmental expenditures and taxation. It is the latter method which is the focus of this paper.

2. It is necessary, of course, to define "economic position." If it is assumed that the individual's purpose as an economic man is to consume, his economic well-being can be defined as his collection of assets which gives claim to consumption (that is, his wealth position) plus the value of goods and services he receives from the government. But the data and measurement techniques concerning wealth are incomplete so that operationally this measure is less than satisfactory. Income can be measured more easily and, to the extent that it varies closely with wealth, a change in income will describe a change in an individual's "economic position." As a proxy for wealth this study utilizes gross income as defined by the Census Bureau [18].

3. Three major problems arise: (1) some products, such as agricultural extension services, are not priced in spite of a demand for them, (2) little is known about education's product, and (3) it is difficult to define an educational production function because (a) basic inputs (i.e., students) differ drastically even within the same institution; (b) little is known about the way in which students learn; and (c) some of the parameters are endogenous to the system (for example, output, which is measured as achievement, is itself a function of achievement). See S. Bowles [3].

4. In all cases it will be assumed that the individual or the state has full information, recognizing that there is a distinction between problems in which the appropriate opportunity cost measure would refer to the best actually perceived alternative versus those in which opportunity costs would refer to an hypothesized optimum that omniscience would identify. See Bowman [4]

5. In the computation of "basic subsidies," research grants and payments for contract work are not included. Standard student costs include tuition and fees, books and supplies, foregone earnings, and room, board and transportation. The basic subsidy does not include scholarships or financial aid grants.

6. By including only the state-supported programs, a large number of loans and grants given to the student are omitted. It should not be inferred, however, that non-state financial aid has no effect on the size of the state's subsidy. To some extent, a removal of all financial aid by sources other than the state government may change the magnitude of state appropriations. Since this study attempts to isolate the distributional effects of a state's financing policy, it is assumed that all levels of non-state support remain constant, and thus the interaction between the size of state and non-state subsidies is not taken into account.

7. See G. M. Vredeveld [20, p. 72] for a description of these awards.

8. See Aaron and von Furstenberg [1] for an application of this analysis to housing subsidies.

9. The efficiency of a subsidy is defined as the value of the subsidy divided by the cost of the subsidy. This measure varies indirectly with the absolute value of the price elasticity and the size of the per unit subsidy.

10. Given the elasticities of demand, the elasticity of substitution (s) and the parameter (p) can be computed since $s = \frac{1}{1 + p}$. D can be found by setting the marginal rate of substitution equal to the price ratio and by substituting $cX_1 = X_2$, where c indicates the relative magnitude of each good consumed initially. One can thus solve for the realized welfare level, U. Removing the subsidy, the price of X_1 will increase by $\$b$ and the welfare level decreases to U_1. The cash-equivalent benefits of the subsidy are found by multiplying the subsidy by the ratio of the percentage decrease in welfare caused by the removal of the subsidy to the cost of the subsidy $(\$bX_1)$ as a percentage of income.

11. The effects of quantity constraints on the amount of education purchased are unknown. They are likely to be very small in the United States since there is probably some institution of higher learning which a student can attend if he has the necessary financial resources. See R. Campbell and B. Siegel [5, p. 488] and M. Blaug [2, pp. 171–72].

12. The percentage of income spent on higher education was estimated to be: 20.14 for families with an income of $0–3,999; 4.95 for the income class $4,000–7,999; 4.31 for income class $8,000–9,999; 4.30 for income class $10,000–14,999; and 1.8 for income class $15,000 and above.

13. The probability of graduating from high school is estimated for each income class by weighting the percentage of family heads 35–44 years of age who have completed high school by the percentage of 20-year-olds who had been graduated from high school by 1969 as reported by the Census Bureau [19]. See G. M. Vredeveld [20, pp. 83–85] for a more complete discussion concerning computation of the distribution parameter.

14. This section on partial taxes draws heavily from Harberger [9] and especially Mieszkowski [12, 13].

15. The output effect discussed above is more broadly defined than Mieszkowski's definition since he does not consider the elasticity of factor substitution as it affects relative price changes due ot the output effect.

16. This output effect will be felt nationally, but primarily by state firms which sell within the state. It is assumed that the quantity demanded of the products of these firms will decrease due to the costs of transporting their goods great distances. It also is assumed that the proceeds of the tax are spent on the same items as private individuals would have purchased.

17. There may be some interrelationships among earmarked and non-earmarked taxes which will cause the rates of earmarked taxes to change with a change of expenditures for education, but it is difficult to determine the direction or magnitude of the change.

18. In 1963 the tax structure in Indiana was changed partly because of demand for local property tax relief. Presently, there are again strong demands for property tax relief and it is conceivable that with a reduction of state expenditures the state government would opt to lower local taxes rather than state taxes. Locally imposed taxes also may be affected by a change in the size of the school operating in its city. Because of the non-tax status of schools, higher education may impose costs on local

governments by removing valuable property from the tax rolls which, in effect, means a municipal subsidy. On the other hand, an expansion of higher education may create locational economies which increase land values in the city and reduce tax rates. If the additional governmental services which are required as a result of the expansion of the university cost less than the additional revenues generated by higher land values, tax rates will decrease.

In addition to the lack of certainty concerning the relationship between municipal taxes and subsidies to education, there is a lack of unanimity concerning the incidence of local taxes. Local governments rely heavily on property taxes as a source of revenue and Dick Netzer [14] argues that the property tax is of the regressive excise variety. Recently, however, Harberger [9] and Mieszkowski [12, 13] have argued that the property tax is essentially a tax on profits. In this case, a property tax is probably more progressive than the incidence of state taxes as a whole. To a large extent the incidence of a property tax depends on the mobility and long-run supply of capital. In brief, property tax incidence is an empirical question which has not yet been resolved.

19. Hansen and Weisbrod [8] argue that this approach implies that if a government's tax structure is progressive, the distribution of tax burdens for the government's expenditure on education is also progressive. A further implication is that if a certain proportion of government's total expenditures is allocated to a given program, every tax-paying group pays the same proportion of its taxes to support that particular program. Hansen and Weisbrod claim that these implications have no logical foundation and therefore the above assumption should not be made.

But unelss one knows *ex ante* the extent to which particular taxes will change with a change in expenditures, some assumptions must be made. The estimate of cost incidence will vary greatly depending on the magnitude of the assumed tax changes. To overcome a wide variance in cost estimates, the assumption of equi-proportional reductions for all taxes, except those two categories mentioned above, will be maintained.

20. Mean Income for all families and unrelated individuals in the state of Indiana is $9,156. See U.S. Bureau of the Census [18].

21. See the discussion of the study by the Jencks' group in the *Harvard Educational Review* [17].

REFERENCES

1. Aaron, H. J. and G. M. von Furstenberg: "The Inefficiency of Transfers in Kind. The Case of Housing Assistance," *Western Economic Journal*, Vol. 9, No. 1, June 1971, pp. 184–91.

2. Blaug, M.: "An Economic Interpretation of the Private Demand for Education," *Economica*, Vol. 33, May 1966, pp. 166–82.

3. Bowles, S.: "Towards an Educational Production Function," in W. L. Hansen, ed., *Education, Income and Human Capital,*

Conference on Education and Income, University of Wisconsin, 1969, New York, National Bureau of Economic Research, 1970, pp. 11–70.

4. Bowman, M. J.: "The Costing of Human Resource Development," in E. Robinson and J. Vaizey, eds., *The Economics of Education*, New York, St. Martin's Press, 1966, Chapter 14, pp. 421–50.

5. Campbell, R. and B. Siegel: "Demand for Higher Education in the United States," *American Economic Review*, Vol. 57, June 1967, pp. 482–94.

6. Galper, H. and R. M. Dunn, Jr.: "A Short-Run Demand Function for Higher Education in the United States," *Journal of Political Economy*, Vol. 77, No. 5, September-October 1969, pp. 765–77.

7. Hansen, W. L. and B. A. Weisbrod: *Benefits, Costs and Finance of Public Higher Education*, Chicago, Markham, 1969.

8. Hansen, W. L. and B. A. Weisbrod: "Who Pays for a Public Expenditure Program?," *National Tax Journal*, Vol. 24, No. 4, December 1971.

9. Harberger, A. C.: "The Incidence of the Corporation Income Tax," *Journal of Political Economy*, Vol. 70, June 1962.

10. Hoenack, S. A.: "The Efficient Allocation of Subsidies to College Students," *American Economic Review*, Vol. 61, No. 3 part 1, June 1971, pp. 302–11.

11. Jencks, C., et. al.: *Inequality: A Reassessment of the Effect of Family and Schooling in America*, New York, Basic Books, 1972.

12. Mieszkowski, P. M.: "On the Theory of Tax Incidence," *Journal of Political Economy*, Vol. 75, June 1967, pp. 250–62.

13. Mieszkowski, P. M.: "Tax Incidence Theory: The Effects of Taxes on the Distribution of Income," *Journal of Economic Literature*, Vol. 7, No. 4, December 1969, pp. 1103–24.

14. Netzer, D.: *Economics of the Property Tax*, Washington, D.C., Brookings, 1966.

15. Ostheimer, R. H.: *Student Charges and Financing Higher Education*, New York, Columbia University Press, 1953.

16. Pechman, J.: "The Distributional Effects of Public Higher Education in California," *Journal of Human Resources,* Vol. 5, Summer 1970, pp. 361–70.
17. "Perspectives on Inequality: A Reassessment of the Effect of Family and Schooling in America," *Harvard Educational Review,* Vol. 43, No. 1, February 1973, pp. 37–164.
18. U.S. Department of Commerce, Bureau of the Census: *General Population Characteristics, Indiana, 1970,* PC(1)-B-16.
19. U.S. Department of Commerce, Bureau of the Census: *Population Characteristics,* Series P-20, No. 206, October 1970.
20. Vredeveld, G. M.: "Income Redistributive Effects of Subsidizing Public Higher Education in Indiana," unpublished doctoral dissertation, Bloomington, Indiana University, 1973.
21. Windham, D. M.: *Education, Equality and Income Redistribution,* Lexington, Massachusetts, Heath, 1970.

APPENDIX

The basic tables upon which the study is based and an explanation of their derivation are presented in this Appendix.

TABLE A-1

General Note: This table includes computation for the state institutions of higher education in Indiana. They are Indiana University-Bloomington (IU-B), Purdue University-Lafayette (PU-L), Ball State University (BSU), Indiana State University (ISU), regional campuses of Indiana and Purdue Universities (IU-R and PU-R), Indiana University-Purdue University at Indianapolis (IUPU-I), Vincennes University (Vin) and Indiana Vocational Technical School (IV Tech). All costs were rounded to the nearest five dollars. Parenthesized figures indicate estimates when no research costs were attributed to students. Sources of data are listed in G. M. Vredeveld [8].

Line *a*: Instructional costs were calculated from the financial reports of each institution. Based on a recent Purdue cost study and earlier state studies analyzing the cost of higher education, it was assumed that the education of a graduate student at PU-L and IU-B was 2.3 times the cost of educating an undergraduate student. For all other schools the costs of educating a graduate student and an undergraduate student were assumed to be the same. One estimate of instructional costs includes costs of fundamental research. The second estimate (shown in parentheses below the first estimate) excludes research costs.

Line *b*: Perfectly competitive markets were assumed such that the expected yield on capital is equal to the market rate of interest. The yield to capital was conceived to consist of three parts: rent,

TABLE A-1
Annual Per Student Costs and Subsidies of
Indiana Public Institutions of Higher Education

	IU-B	PU-L	BSU	ISU	IU-R	IUPU-I	PU-R	Vin	IV Tech
a) Instruction	$1525 (1345)	$1755 (1515)	$1525	$1490	$1205	$1205	$1200	$1045	
b) Capital									
i) Land	10	10	10	10	15	10	20	10	
ii) Buildings	190	240	185	140	155	165	140	140	
iii) Equipment	125	190	105	90	75	80	80	45	
c) Subtotal of a and b	1850 (1670)	2195 (1955)	1825	1730	1450	1460	1440	1240	
d) Books and Supplies	200	200	200	200	200	200	200	200	
e) Room, Board, and Transportation	475	475	450	450	200	100	200	225	
f) Foregone Earnings	4000	4000	4000	4000	4000	4000	4000	4000	
g) Total Cost (sum of a, b, d, e, and f)	6525 (6345)	6870 (6630)	6475	6380	5700	5655	5840	5665	
h) Tuition and fees paid by student	530	570	430	410	600	600	600	580	300
i) Costs borne by private non-student sources and by federal government	5	5	0	0	0	0	0	0	
j) State Subsidy (equal to g minus the sum of d, e, f, h, and i)	1315 (1135)	1620 (1380)	1395	1320	850	860	840	660	770

appreciation (depreciation) in the real value of capital, and appreciation (depreciation) in capital's value due to inflation. In owning capital, the school foregoes only the rent and this is used as a proxy for the cost. Annual rent was assumed to be equal to the annual yield of the capital (i) plus the capital depreciation rate (d) or $i + d$. For land the annual rent was estimated at 3% (9%−6%) of current land value. For buildings it was estimated to be $.075B_C + (B_R/40 - .035B_C)$ where replacement value (B_R) was found by using the construction costs reported by *Boeckh Building Cost Modifier* [2], current value (B_C) of buildings was calculated by using straight line depreciation over 40 years, and where .075 and .035 reflect the interest rate and expected inflationary rate respectively. It was assumed that the building cost index and the general price index moved in direct proportion to each other. Replacement costs for equipment (E_R) were estimated by $E_P(1 + .035)^A$ where E_P is purchase price, A is the average age of equipment, and .035 represents the expected rate of annual inflation. Current value of equipment (E_C) was found by using straight line depreciation of E_R over ten years. Annual rent (cost) of equipment was calculated as: $.075E_C + (E_R/10 - .035E_C)$.

Line d: All expenses for books and supplies as estimated by the College Entrance Examination Board [3] were included as costs.

Line e: Only the costs for room, board and transportation which exceed the cost of these services if the individual were not to purchase education were calculated in this category. These additional costs borne by students living away from home were assumed to be one half of the total room, board, and transportation expenses, or approximately $500. The cost estimates in line e are a result of weighting $500 by the proportion of non-commuters attending the individual schools.

Line f: Following Becker [1], the value of time foregone for educational purposes was calculated by estimating the value of the time spent at the expense of work and also the time which would have been used for leisure. It was assumed that the student devotes forty hours a week to his academic duties, the value of which was estimated to be $4,000 annually. Income received from part-time employment was not deducted from earnings foregone since it is assumed that the individual had the option to take on a part-time job regardless of whether or not he was in school.

Line *h*: Tuition and fees exclude that portion paid for non-academic purposes—for example, health services, athletic programs, student unions, and convocation or concert series.

Line *i*: This estimate includes only those gifts or grants which the university received to operate "educational" programs. Contract grants, financial aid, etc. were not included.

TABLE A-2

General Note: The distribution of students by income class for all schools except Vincennes and I.V. Tech is based on the *Family Income Survey* [4]. This study was based on a ten percent sample of all Indiana residents attending those schools. The distribution of students for Vincennes and for I.V. Tech is based on data supplied by those schools. Total number of students is taken from H.E.W. [6]. A part-time student was counted as one-half a full-time student.

Column *11*: This column is equal to the weighted sum of Columns *2* through *10*.

TABLE A-3

General Note: The parenthesized figure indicates the estimate of subsidies when research costs were not attributed to students. Total subsidies received by each income class are obtained by multiplying the per student subsidy received at each school times the number of students attending that school in each particular income class.

TABLE A-4

Columns *2* and *3*: Includes all state grants at all campuses for each school.

Column *4*: Only the State Scholarship Commission's grants are included in ISU's totals.

Column *6*: Data concerning the distribution of grants by income

TABLE A-2

Distribution of Full Time Equivalent (FTE)
Indiana Students by Income Class and School
(in percentages)
Fall, 1969

(1) Gross Income Class	(2) IU-B	(3) PU-L	(4) BSU	(5) ISU	(6) IU-R	(7) IUPU-I	(8) PU-R	(9) Vin	(10) IV Tech	(11) All Schools
$ 0- 2,999	.019	.018	.027	.030	.009	.033	.018	.106	.100	.208
3,000- 5,999	.051	.066	.068	.088	.100	.074	.035	.105	.156	.074
6,000- 7,499	.047	.042	.071	.092	.063	.060	.044	.145	.151	.067
7,500- 8,999	.053	.066	.081	.083	.074	.107	.094	.141	.178	.082
9,000-11,999	.135	.183	.200	.209	.179	.244	.313	.212	.228	.193
12,000-14,999	.171	.163	.211	.214	.191	.210	.206	.104	.078	.182
15,000-19,999	.183	.180	.196	.169	.141	.173	.210	.105	.079	.171
20,000+	.343	.281	.144	.113	.244	.098	.081	.041	.030	.202
total number FTE undergrads	18,120	14,016	12,199	11,578	8,321	6,721	4,232	2,758	3,881	81,826

TABLE A-3

"Basic" Subsidies to Students Attending
Indiana Institutions of Public Higher Education
by Income Class
1969-70

Gross Income Class	Subsidy
$ 0- 2,999	$ 2,587,585 (2,465,185)
3,000- 5,999	5,974,170 (5,585,850)
6,000- 7,499	5,902,460 (5,608,220)
7,500- 8,999	6,347,860 (5,921,200)
9,000-11,999	18,826,590 (17,770,710)
12,000-14,999	18,357,215 (17,649,815)
15,000-19,999	17,540,355 (16,162,040)
20,000+	21,344,160 (19,411,840)
Total	$96,880,395 (90,574,860)

TABLE A-4

Money Value of Scholarships Supported
by State of Indiana
Distributed by Income Class
1969-70

(1) Gross Income Class	(2) IU[1]	(3) PU[1]	(4) ISU[2]	(5) VIN	(6) Total[3]
$ 0- 2,999	$ 98,650	$104,345	$15,552	$14,840	$ 233,387
3,000- 5,999	317,332	204,569	50,101	17,565	589,567
6,000- 7,499	296,258	137,724	29,612	8,809	472,403
7,500- 8,999	222,021	150,680	11,232	8,809	392,742
9,000-11,999	494,869	319,371	8,682	3,534	826,456
12,000-14,999	256,337	175,449	175	0	431,961
15,000-19,999	101,121	91,461	576	0	193,158
20,000+	22,221	16,951	0	0	39,172

class were not available for Ball State University and are not in-cluded in the total. Indiana Vocational Technical School received no state scholarship money in 1969–70.

TABLE A-5

General Note: This table is based on results of Mundel [5] who used the 1967 Survey of Economic Opportunity to find the number of students in each income class who qualified as dependents under IRS rules.

Columns *1* and *2*: These columns were derived by interpolating Mundel's data [5, p. 300] in order to coincide with the income classification shown in Column *1*.

Column *5*: The total number of Indiana students by income class is found by applying the percentage distribution of all Indiana students by income class (Column *11, *Table *A-2*) to the total number of Indana students.

Column *7*: Indiana tax laws allow a family a $500 exemption for each dependent who is not a spouse or taxpayer. Payments for the income tax (levied at a rate of 2% of income) were calculated for all income classes using the average number of dependents and parents in each income class given by the *Family Income Survey.* On the basis of these calculations it was found that the dependency allow-ance was of no value for the lowest income class but amounted to a tax savings of $10 per student ($500 × 2%) for all other income classes.

TABLE A-6

Source: Indiana Department of Commerce: *Indiana Fact Book,* Economic Research Division, Indianapolis, October 1971.

TABLE A-7

Column *2*: Based on the assumptions described on pages 16 and 17, tax burdens can be expected to depend on the pattern of con-sumption as well as on labor income and land ownership. The burden of the sales tax is distributed in the following way: 55% distributed according to expenditures on taxable consumption, 40% according to wage earning and 5% according to income from land. The consumption patterns, dividends received, and wages of income classes were taken from the U.S Labor Department's *Survey of Consumer Expenditures* 1960–61 [7]. These data were adjusted by Mr. Donald Kiefer of the Indiana State Commission on Taxation, Indianapolis, to reflect inflation in prices and wages.

Column 3: Indiana's corporation gross income tax is essentially a transaction or turnover tax. It is levied on gross receipts derived from the intra-state sale of services and property at the rate of 2% and 0.5% respectively. Although the cumulative rate of the tax depends on the degree of integration in the industry, the lack of data necessitated treating all industry as paying the same rate. The burden of this tax was distributed in the same way as the sales tax except that 55% was distributed by expenditures on total consumption rather than by expenditures on sales-taxable consumption.

Column 4: The incidence of the personal income tax was found by distributing the receipts from the tax by taxable income. The sales tax credit against income tax liability was allowed in calculating income tax receipts and was not taken into account in finding the incidence of the sales tax. Although this does not change the incidence of the aggregate of taxes, it may overstate the regressivity (progressivity) of the sales (individual income) tax.

Column 5: It was assumed that the full burden of this tax was passed on to purchasers of insurance. Approximately 50% of the insurance sold in Indiana was purchased by businesses who, it was assumed, passed the cost of insurance forward to the price of their product. It was assumed that the other half was borne by private individuals. Therefore, one-half of the insurance tax was distributed according to insurance purchases and the other half according to total consumption.

Columns 6 and 7: The burden of these taxes was distributed among income classes in proportion to their consumption of these items.

Column 8: The intangibles tax is levied at the rate of .25% on intangibles such as stocks, bonds, and out-of-state bank accounts.

TABLE A-5

Tax Exemptions as Educational Subsidies

(1) Gross Income Class	(2) Number of Qualifying Students	(3) Number of Students	(4) Percentage of Students who Qualify (Col. 2/Col. 3)	(5) Total Number of Indiana Students	(6) Total Number of Indiana Students Who Qualify (Col. 4 X Col. 5)	(7) Per Student Tax Savings	(8) Total Tax Savings (Col. 6 X Col. 7)
$ 0- 2,999	232,831	263,195	.885	1,921	1,700	$ 0	$ 0
3,000- 5,999	413,558	661,470	.625	5,851	3,657	10	36,570
5,000- 7,499	251,568	647,544	.388	5,065	1,965	10	19,650
7,500- 8,999	283,568	686,536	.413	6,463	2,669	10	26,690
9,000-11,999	698,908	1,076,734	.649	16,681	10,826	10	108,260
12,000-14,999	748,795	909,068	.824	16,418	13,528	10	135,280
15,000-19,999	505,660	623,870	.811	15,807	12,819	10	128,190
20,000+	458,593	701,854	.653	18,951	12,375	10	123,750
Total	3,593,481	5,570,271		81,826	59,539		$578,390

TABLE A-6

Tax Sources of Indiana State

General Fund Revenues in Fiscal Year 1969-70

Tax	Revenue
1. Sales	.$214,758,939
2. Corporate Income	.167,979,854
3. Individual Income	.216,384,250
4. Insurance	.23,962,459
5. Alcoholic Beverage	.10,113,011
6. Cigarette	.16,612,822
7. Intangibles	.1,968,419
8. Privilege and Occupation	.4,545,592
9. Inheritance and Estate	.15,013,311
Total Tax Revenue	.$671,338,647

This tax was distributed in proportion to the dividends received by income class.

Column *9*: The privilege and occupation taxes include licensing fees for a wide variety of businesses. They are lump-sum taxes and, in the short run, do not affect output or prices. However, under long-run competitive conditions, these taxes will be passed forward to the price of the product. Under conditions of monopoly they will be borne by the owners of capital. It was assumed that 50% of these taxes are passed forward and thus that portion was distributed according to the total consumption by income classes. The burden of the other half of these taxes was assumed to fall on owners of capital and was distributed according to dividend income.

Column *10*: Indiana imposes an inheritance tax at progressive rates on the recipients of inherited property. Although most of the total value of property is bequeathed by individuals with large incomes, their income level should not be used as a proxy for the income level of the beneficiary. If it is assumed that there is a strong correlation between family income and the income of immediate re-

TABLE A-7

Distribution of Taxes Paid
by Income Class
Fiscal Year 1969-70

(1) Gross Income Class	(2) Sales	(3) Corp. Income	(4) Indiv. Income	(5) Insurance	(6) Alcoh. Bev.	(7) Cigarette	(8) Intangibles	(9) Prov., Occup.	(10) Inher., Estate	(11) Total
$ 0- 2,999	.0369	.0370	.0028	.0415	.0317	.0680	.0070	.0545	.0070	.0257
3,000- 5,999	.0917	.0919	.0496	.1007	.1097	.1562	.0290	.1206	.0290	.0775
6,000- 7,499	.0677	.0678	.0541	.0759	.0841	.0989	.0286	.0767	.0286	.0654
7,500- 8,999	.0991	.0987	.0907	.0948	.0831	.1208	.0275	.1136	.0275	.0929
9,000-11,999	.2005	.2011	.1961	.1857	.1928	.2199	.0571	.1384	.0571	.1915
12,000-14,999	.1697	.1700	.1851	.1699	.1752	.1234	.0720	.1733	.0720	.1681
15,000-19,999	.1238	.1755	.1971	.1731	.1763	.1451	.1069	.1794	.1069	.1765
20,000+	.2085	.1579	.2254	.1583	.1471	.0676	.6719	.1435	.6719	.2024
Total	1.0000	1.0000	1.0000	1.0000	1.0000	1.0000	1.0000	1.0000	1.0000	1.0000

latives and if most gifts accrue to immediate relatives, the average income of the recipient of inheritances is likely to be above average. In order to reflect the probability that recipients come from higher income groups, the burden of this tax was distributed according to the distribution of dividends received by income class.

Column *11*: This column is a weighted average of the respective rows in Columns 2–10.

APPENDIX REFERENCES

1. Becker, G. S.: *Human Capital,* New York, Columbia University Press, 1964.
2. *Boeckh Building Cost Modifier,* Milwaukee, American Appraisal Company, March-April 1970.
3. College Entrance Examination Board, "A Letter to Parents," Princeton, 1971.
4. *Family Income Survey,* unpublished report, Financial Aid Office, Purdue University, 1971.
5. Mundel, D. S.: "Federal Aid to Higher Education and the Poor," unpublished doctoral dissertation, Cambridge, M.I.T., 1971.
6. U.S. Department of Health, Education and Welfare, Office of Education: *Fall Enrollment in Higher Education 1969 Supplementary Information,* Higher Education Surveys Branch, Washington, D.C., Government Printing Office, 1971.
7. U.S. Department of Labor: *Survey of Consumer Expenditures 1960–1961,* Bureau of Labor Statistics Report No. 237093, Supplement 3, Part A, Washington, D.C., U.S. Government Printing Office, May 1966.
8. Vredeveld, G. M.: "Income Redistributive Effects of Subsidizing Public Higher Education in Indiana," unpublished doctoral dissertation, Bloomington, Indiana University, 1973.

Comments on "Income Inequality and Subsidizing Higher Education"

Gerald Sirkin*

These estimates of the distribution of subsidies and costs of undergraduate education have been prepared with admirable care and attention to detail. I shall confine my comments to a few broad questions.

1. The finding that, in one government program, there is some redistribution from the lower-middle income groups to the upper income groups should not surprise us. The components of a government budget are not determined by a series of separate decisions, but as parts of a package. To put together a coalition that will approve the package, different parts of it will have to appeal to different groups, and the subsidization of higher education may be one of the inducements thrown to the upper half of the income scale. Examining how the package is assembled is informative, but for distributional analysis, it is the whole package that counts.

2. The findings about distribution in this study depend heavily on the assumptions made with respect to the sales tax and the corporation gross income tax, which being essentially a transactions tax, is treated in the same way as the sales tax. These two taxes make up about two-thirds of the total taxes to be allocated.

One assumption—that capital is mobile and labor is relatively immobile—leads to a second assumption, that 40% of these two taxes are shifted backward to wage earnings. I see no persuasive grounds for those assumptions, which contribute substantially to the regressivity of the tax structure in this study.

The alleged regressivity of the sales tax should be questioned for another, and more fundamental, reason. The conclusion that the sales tax when shifted forward is regressive rests on the decline of the average propensity to consume with the rise of income, as found in budget data. So far as I know, no one has challenged this ancient orthodoxy. Yet modern analysis of consumption has shown

*Professor of Economics, City College of the City University of New York.

how misleading budget data can be and has suggested that, with re-spect to lifetime income, an average propensity to consume equal to one, at all income levels, may be a reasonable approximation to re-ality. If lifetime income is all consumed (or, more generally, if con-sumption is proportional to lifetime income) a completely general sales tax would be a proportional tax, and a sales tax which ex-empts products (like food) which are a larger proportion of lower income budgets would be a progressive tax.

3. While subsidies for college education may not involve any sig-nificant redistribution between income groups, they do result in redistribution within income groups. Families which do not send children to college contribute to families which do. The inequity of that type of redistribution, together with the "waste" associated with any subsidy, of which this paper reminds us, means that these sub-sidies can be justified only by a showing of compensatory external benefits. Such a showing seems improbable; indeed, the exter-nalities, on balance, might well be negative.

7

On the Allocation of Resources and the Training of Manpower in a University

Problems which revolve around efficient resource allocation have always been a major concern of economists. It is, therefore, ironic that economists employed in academic institutions have seldom turned their attention to the internal resource allocation of the institutions for whom they toil—the universities. This paper describes a linear programming model applicable to any public university which generates explicit quantitative information about: (1) the optimal allocation of resources inside the university;[1] (2) the shadow price attached to each input used in the academic process; and, (3) the optimal mixture of academic outputs produced by the university. While the model is applied to Illinois State University and those results are reported here, the model is general in nature and is designed to assist any academic decision-maker at any university in making efficient use of the limited resources available to him.[2] Further, the model should increase the sensitivity of the university to manpower problems outside the university.

I. THE UNDERLYING ASSUMPTIONS

The model which is developed here is amenable to a wide range of assumptions about the academic process. The assumptions upon which this particular application of the model has been based are:

*Associate Professor of Economics, Illinois State University. The author is indebted to Dean Richard Bond, Dean Milton Greenberg, Dr. Warren Harden, and Mr. John Sealock for assistance given to the study which is reported in this paper.

(1) The university may be visualized as a multiproduct firm.
(2) The outputs of the university are the graduates of its many programs.[3]
(3) The value of the university's outputs to society may be approximated by the present discounted value of the change in the lifetime income streams of the students who obtain education at the university.
(4) The external effects of higher education are in net terms negligible in size.[4]
(5) Public expenditures on higher education may be viewed as an investment in human capital.[5]
(6) The public university should seek to maximize the difference between the value of its graduates which is attributable to higher education and the cost of educating its graduates.[6]

While the above assumptions contain within them elements of controversy, these controversies have been discussed in detail elsewhere,[7] and those discussions will not be duplicated here. It will suffice to mention that the assumptions made here are typical of those made in studies of the economics of education and are not unique to the work reported here.

II. *THE MODEL*

The linear programming model upon which this study is based involved the maximization of a linear objective function of the following form:

$$a = P_1X_1 + P_2X_2 + \ldots + P_nX_n$$

where X_j = subdivisions of the college or university such as departments, etc., measured in terms of the number of student graduates.

P_j = "profit per unit" on the output of the subdivision (discussed below).

The above linear function was maximized subject to a series of constraints stated in the form of linear inequalities:

$$a_{11}X_1 + a_{12}X_2 + \ldots + a_{1n}X_n \leq K_1$$

$$a_{21}X_1 + a_{22}X_2 + \ldots + a_{2n}X_n \leq K_2$$

$$a_{m1}X_1 + a_{m2}X_2 + \ldots + a_{mn}X_n \leq K_m$$

$$X_j^* \geq \cdot 75X_j$$

where X_j = subdivisions of the college or university measured in terms of the number of student graduates.

X_j^* = quantity of X_j in optimal solution.

K_i = input constraints which constrain the activities of the subdivision, e.g., the limitation of the university's budget input.

a_{ij} = coefficients of the X_j based on technical information such as student-faculty ratios, etc.

The basic model, then, seeks to maximize the "total profit" which the university realizes on its multiple outputs to society. Such constraining factors as budget limitations, space limitations, required student-faculty ratios, available computer time, etc., provide definite boundaries for the problem. Further, in order to enhance realism and applicability, no individual output (X_j) is allowed to decrease by more than 25 per cent of its previous value in the optimal solution. This constraint recognizes practical political factors and indicates that institutional stability must be maintained.

Associated with every linear programming problem is a companion problem known as a "dual" problem. Dual problems often yield important results. So also it is in this case. The dual problem will generate "shadow prices" for each input used by the university; the shadow price is the imputed value at the margin of each input to the academic process. In this model, the shadow price tells us the net addition to the total value generated by the university which is obtained when an extra unit of a given input, for example, computer services, is utilized. The shadow prices, then, are the value of the marginal product of the inputs used in the academic process. A positive shadow price indicates that all of the available units of a given input (for example, history teachers) were used in the optimal solution. A zero shadow price indicates that some units of the input which were available were not used in the optimal solution. Such information may be used by academic administrators as a guide to where increments or decrements in avialable resources should be applied. Both the original or "primal" problem and the dual[8] problem were solved in the course of this study.

The Meaning of the P_j's (Profits Per Unit)

The P_j's, profits per unit on the university's outputs to society, are the estimated productivity attributable to a student's collegiate education minus the estimated costs of educating that student. This statement, however, invites further discussion. Presumably, each output of the university affects the productivity of society in a non-negligible fashion. But, it is not the total productivity of the university graduate that is of interest to this study; rather, it is the *net* increment to the productivity of society due the university education of the individual that is of importance in this model. This model considers the lifetime income stream of a student to be an appropriate proxy for that student's productivity. Not all of this lifetime stream of income may be attributed to the beneficient effects of the university, however. From the flow of income associated with any given year in the student's lifetime must be subtracted the following: (1) the income which would have been earned anyway by the student had he not attained a collegiate education; (2) the income which is attributable not to education, but rather to differential student ability and motivation; and, (3) an adjustment which recognizes the fact that not all college graduates remain in the labor force throughout their lifetimes and, therefore, do not earn income in certain years.

Following Hansen and Weisbrod [13] and others, adjustment (1) above will be approximated by the U.S. Census-reported earnings of individuals whose education terminated with high school. Adjustment (2) above will be assumed to be 25 per cent of the observed differential in earnings between college and high school graduates. That is, only 75 per cent of the observed differential will be attributed to the collegiate education. Although several alternative per cent adjustments have been used in other studies,[9] the thrust of recent research supports the 25 per cent adjustment.[10] Adjustment (3) above will be a variable per cent and will reflect the fact that some individuals die or leave the labor force[11] and, therefore, do not earn each year the incomes that are reported as accruing to college graduates in a given field. This particular adjustment has great significance with respect to women and is an important reason why net profits per unit will vary between disciplines.

On the cost side of the picture, it is readily obvious that the direct costs the university expends to educate an individual must be considered. Such expenses as faculty salaries, physical maintenance costs, and the like are relevant. Additionally, if one identifies the university as being the agent of society, and dependent upon and responsible to society, then one must also include as a cost of higher education the foregone income of the student who is attending the university. This is because the student who attends the university is not (to some degree) in the labor force producing product for society. Society loses this product. This foregone product, as measured by the foregone student income,[12] represents an opportunity cost to society and must be included if it is to be said that the university operates in behalf of society.[13]

We can, therefore, write:

$$\text{Profit Per Unit} = \sum_{t=1}^{N} \frac{(\$_t^c - \$_t^c (.75)\ (A_t) - C_t)}{(1 + r)^t}$$

Profit so defined is, of course, an accounting concept and is not actually realized by the university, although one may argue that it is realized by society in the form of a net increment to society's product. It is appropriately viewed as being a social profit and should not be confused with private profits.

A Closer Look at the Constraints

It is crucially important that all of the short-run constraints[14] which the university faces be incorporated into the model. If binding constraints are excluded from consideration, the resulting answers may be of dubious value. In addition to reflecting the obvious limitations of budget, faculty, students, space,[15] equipment, etc., the constraint inequalities must also take into account three other factors. First, the output of each department depends upon inputs from other departments. Each department or division services other departments or divisions by offering courses, providing materials, and the like. That is, a college graduate in biology conventionally takes courses in English, sociology, art, and a host of other disciplines. Hence, the production of a biology major at the baccalaureate level requires inputs from other disciplines.

Second, some areas of the university (for example, the computer center) will earn no profits whatsoever in the sense the term is used here, because the sole purpose of such areas is to provide necessary intermediate inputs for other areas of the university. The constraint equations must reflect the necessity (if it exists) for those inputs to be included in the outputs of the various areas of the university that do earn profits.

Third, breaking down the university's output into chemistry majors, psychology majors, etc., is necessary but not sufficient detail for the model. Great differences exist between a Ph.D. graduate in chemistry and a B.A. graduate in chemistry. The differences appear not only in earning power, but also in cost of education. Separate outputs must be used to reflect these differences. Further, the distinction must be made between students in teacher education programs and those who are in non-teacher education programs. The market for teachers is often substantially different from the market for other university graduates. Also, the amounts of resources devoted to each type of education often differ.

Both the objective function and the constraint inequalities, then, must adequately represent the above interdependencies of outputs as well as differentiate sufficiently the multiple products being produced. Further, the constraints must reflect the educational wisdom, or lack thereof, of the decision-makers in each area of the university. For example, if a given department insists that no class enrollment exceed 20, then so be it. The constraints will reflect this judgment, and the optimal solution will reflect this desire as well as the fact that this particular department's output may be expensive to produce.

A difficulty which arises with respect to the constraints is that a public university is often subject to various constraints of a sociological or cultural nature. It is usually not possible to reflect such factors in the form of a linear inequality. However, certain of these constraining factors are implicitly included in the model via the objective equation which (because it is partially based upon the workings of the market) approximates the needs, desires, and tastes of society and via the constraints which reflect society's willingness to fund certain types of educational ventures. Hence, society, via the marketplace, will have some influence on both the coefficients and the selection of outputs in the objective equation.

The Rate of Discount

The model described here uses as the societal benefit measure the present discounted value of lifetime income streams. Some rate of discount must therefore be specified. A long and involved discussion over what is the correct rate of discount has occured in recent years. Baumol [4], however, has pointed out that there is no single rate of discount that is "correct." The results reported in this paper are based upon a rate of discount of 6 per cent. This choice can be attacked or defended with great vigor in light of competing sets of assumptions that are most attractive.[16] The most intelligent approach would appear to involve the use of several alternative discount rates in order to determine if the empirical results are sensitive to the magnitude of the discount rate. This procedure was followed in this study, but few differences in results were uncovered because of changes in the rate of discount.

Summarizing the Output of the Model and the Model's Implications

The linear programming model[17] generates the optimal solution of X_j's, which represent that collection of university graduates which will maximize the university's net contribution to society's productivity given the constraints the university faces. The solution values of the X_j's indicate which of the university's academic outputs should increase in quantity, be held constant, or be contracted. The optimal pattern of usage of the K_i's, the inputs, is also given. Hence, the model indicates how much of a given input (for example, classroom space) is needed in order for the university to produce the optimal combination of outputs. It should once again be noted that the model was constrained such that no contraction in any given output (for example, English teachers) could be more than 25 per cent in the optimal solution. This constraint was imposed in order to represent political inertia inside the university and the need for some minimum amount of institutional stability.

Finally, the model generates shadow prices which indicate the marginal worth of an extra unit of any input to the academic process. This information can be used to change the quantities of various inputs (for example, secretarial help) that are purchased by the university.

III. *THE DATA AND THE EMPIRICAL RESULTS*

The primary sources of data for the lifetime income streams of college graduates which are a necessary input for the model have been the National Science Foundation [2], the Midwest College Placement Association [3], and the Illinois State University Placement Bureau. These data ordinarily consist of a cross-sectional view of the students' lifetime income streams.

It has been alleged by some economists [10], [21] that the use of cross-sectional data is fraught with danger because it forces the researcher to examine many different cohorts of individuals rather than centering attention on one cohort of individuals through the passage of time. Each successive cohort of individuals may differ from previous cohorts in important ways, for example in the quality of the education given them. As a result, more recent cohorts may have age-earning profiles quite dissimilar to that of older cohorts. Hence, a cross-sectional analysis will not properly reflect the true return to an investment in education by a given individual or cohort. While this argument may have some validity, at least four reasons militate against its acceptance. First, earnings differentials have been remarkably constant in recent decades and this fact would seem to deny the importance of changing cohorts. Second, present discounted values (such as those computed in this study) are fairly insensitive to changes in age-income profiles which occur several years after the discounting procedure has already begun. Thus, even if cohorts do change as time passes, the discounting process will seriously shrink the impact of any such changes upon the empirical results. Third, unlike time series data, cross-sectional data is not as susceptible to the effects of exogenous factors such as the business cycle and full-scale war. Finally, it need be noted only parenthetically that extensive data which detail age, education, income, and academic major are simply not available in time series form.

The empirical portions of the cost, enrollment, space, and other data needed to formulate the constraints in the model were supplied by the Office of Institutional Research at Illinois State University. Other relevant data were taken from the Illinois State University Internal Budget for the academic year 1969–1970.

While the empirical results are based upon cost, enrollment, space and other relationships relevant to Illinois State University for the academic year 1969–1970, the earnings and income data are in most cases not peculiar to Illinois State University and, instead, consists of nationwide profiles of the incomes of college graduates in various fields.[18] The assumption, then, is that the nationwide data accurately reflect the earnings and labor market experiences of graduates of Illinois State University.

Tables *1* and *2* summarize the empirical results of the linear programming model in a qualitative sense.[19] It is apparent from Table *1* that the optimal solution of academic outputs at Illinois State University generally involved a decrease in the output of students trained to teach. This is the major manpower implication of the findings.

It is interesting to note that the staff of the Board of Higher Education for the State of Illinois independently recommended a reduction of 10 per cent in Illinois State University's production of graduates trained to teach. While the Board Staff did not utilize a linear programming model to arrive at its recommendation, it is apparent that the Board Staff explicitly considered market conditions in arriving at its conclusions. [19]

It should be noted, nevertheless, that some academic programs (for example, non-teaching agriculture) were contracted in the optimal solution despite not being connected to teacher education. When a contraction was recommended for any particular programs by the optimal solution, this typically meant one or more of the following circumstances was true: (1) the graduates of the program were not in great demand; (2) the cost of the program was great; (3) the demands of the program for non-monetary input support (for example, space) were large; (4) the program did not service other academic programs as a required course or as a frequently elected optional course and therefore gained no support from other programs; (5) the program services (via its course offerings) other academic programs which also contracted in the optimal solution.

Table 2 summarizes the empirical results as they pertain to selected inputs in the academic process. The results have not been reported for all inputs used in the academic process because the usage of certain inputs (for example, the comptroller's office or the heating plant) does not depend in any substantial way upon the mixture of academic outputs produced by the university. The resources devoted to the comptroller's office are simply not responsive to marginal changes in the composition of the academic outputs of the university. The use of certain inputs, however, is responsive to the actual mixture of outputs. The resources devoted to the Office of the Dean of College of Education decline in the optimal solution because the size of the College of Education declined in the optimal solution.

A zero shadow price for any input means that in the optimal solution not all units of that input currently available would be used. A positive shadow price for an input means that all of the units of that input currently available would be used if the optimal solution of outputs were produced by the university. While the absolute magnitude of the shadow prices is not given, the higher the shadow price, the more valuable to the academic process an extra unit of that input would be if the optimal solution were imposed.

It has been pointed out previously that departments are interdependent in that they service each other's students with coursework.

The Department of Psychology at Illinois State University is heavily involved in servicing students in teacher education programs. Because the optimal output of the model specified a reduction in most types of teacher education outputs, the need for the service input provided by the Department of Psychology declines when the optimal output solution is obeyed.

Of some interest is the evaluation of space needs and usage in the optimal solution. A zero shadow price was generated for both instructional (classroom) space and office space. This implies that sufficient space exists in these two categories despite the complaints of both faculty and administration concerning a shortage of these inputs. On the other hand, laboratory space would be extremely scarce if the dictates of the optimal solution of academic outputs were followed.

While many caveats are associated with the implementation of this model at any given university, one in particular must be mentioned. The model treats the stock of a given type of input as if all units of that input were identical in quality and/or skill. This, of course, need not be so. For example, the quality of all faculty offices is not uniform. Hence, when the model indicates that sufficient faculty office space is available in the optimal solution, this is true, but may imply that some faculty members are using office space which is of low quality.

The results of the model which have been described here relate only to a particular time period—1969–1970. As labor market conditions, budgets, space, academic requirements, and input supplies and prices change, the optimal solution will change. The model must be continuously updated, perhaps on an annual basis, in order to make intelligent use of the results it generates.

IV. *SUMMARY AND CONCLUSIONS*

This paper has described the application of a linear programming model to the process of resource allocation at Illinois State University. The model is designed to assist academic administrators in allocating the scarce resources at their disposal and to make the university more sensitive to labor market conditions. The model, and the assumptions upon which it is based, may be altered to suit the particular decision criteria of a particular academic institution.

The model developed here maximized an objective function which was the total net social profit on the university's academic outputs. This objective function was maximized subject to a myriad of constraints which reflected the limitations of budget, space, and other scarce inputs. Further, the constraints reflected the joint interdependency of many parts of the university. For example, an economics major typically takes coursework in mathematics. Hence, the production of the Economics Department depends upon the production of the Department of Mathematics. The constraints also were reflective of the particular educational delivery system imposed by a given department. Thus, a departmental limitation on class size was reflected in the constraints. The outputs of the model include the optimal mixture of academic outputs by the university; the optimal distribution and usage of inputs inside the university; and, the shadow price of each input.

While the linear programming model developed is general and can be applied to any univeristy, it was applied to Illinois State University in this paper. In the case used for illustrative purposes, the model recommended a substantial reduction in emphasis upon teacher education at Illinois State University.

TABLE 1

A SUMMARY OF THE EMPIRICAL RESULTS CONCERNING
ACADEMIC PROGRAMS GENERATED BY
A LINEAR PROGRAMMING MODEL
OF ILLINOIS STATE UNIVERSITY

KEY: + means that this program should be expanded in size;
     − means that this program should be contracted from 0 to 25 per cent in size;
     −− means that this program should be contracted 25 per cent in size;
     N.C. means that no change in the size of this program is indicated by the model

DEPARTMENT OR AREA	DEGREE PROGRAM	RECOMMENDATION OF MODEL
Biology*	B.S.	+
	B.S., teacher educ.	−
	M.S.	−
	Ph.D.	−
Chemistry	B.S.	+
	B.S., teacher educ.	−
	M.S.	−
Economics	B.S.	+
	M.S.	+
English	B.A.	−−
	B.A., teacher educ.	−−
	M.A.	−−
Foreign Languages**	B.A.	−
	B.A., teacher educ.	−
	M.A.	−−
Geography-Geology	B.S.	+
	B.S., teacher educ.	−
	M.S.	+
History	B.A.	−−
	B.A., teacher educ.	−−
	M.A.	−−
Library Science	B.S., teacher educ.	+

DEPARTMENT OR AREA	DEGREE PROGRAM	RECOMMENDATION OF MODEL
Mathematics	B.S.	+
	B.S., teacher educ.	−
	M.S.	−
Philosophy	B.A.	−
Physics	B.S.	+
	B.S., teacher educ.	−
	M.S.	+
Political Science	B.S.	+
	B.S., teacher educ.	−
	M.S.	+
Psychology	B.S.	+
	B.S., teacher educ.	−
	M.S.	+
Social Sciences	B.S., teacher educ.	−−
	M.S.	−−
Sociology-Anthropology***	B.S.	+
	B.S., teacher educ.	−
	M.S.	+
Speech****	B.S.	+
	B.S., teacher educ.	−
	M.S.	−
Agriculture	B.S.	−−
	B.S., teacher educ.	−−
Home Economics	B.S.	−
	B.S., teacher educ.	−−
	M.S.	−
Industrial Technology	B.S.	+
	B.S., teacher educ.	N.C.
	M.S.	+
Health and Physical Education (Men's)	B.S., teacher educ.	−
	M.S.	−
Health and Physical Education (Women's)	B.S., teacher educ.	−
	M.S.	−

Education	B.S., elementary educ.	–
	M.S.	––
	Ed.D.	+
Educational	M.S.	+
Administration	Ed.D.	+
	Ph.D.	+
Special Education	B.S., teacher educ.	+
	M.S.	+
Art	B.S.	–
	B.S., teacher educ.	–
	M.S.	–
	Ed.D.	N.C.
Music	B.S.	–
	B.S., teacher educ.	–
	M.S.	–

*   includes health related professions at undergraduate level.
**   includes French, German, Latin, Russian, and Spanish majors.
***   includes undergraduate Social Work.
****   includes Speech-Communications, Speech Audiology-Pathology, and Theatre majors.

TABLE 2

A SUMMARY OF EMPIRICAL RESULTS CONCERNING SELECTED
INPUTS TO ACADEMIC PROGRAMS GENERATED BY A LINEAR
PROGRAMMING MODEL OF ILLINOIS STATE UNIVERSITY

KEY: +   means that the shadow price for this input is positive and that extra units of this input could
           be utilized if the optimal solution of outputs were produced;
      0   means that the shadow price of this input is zero and that some of the current stock of units of
           this input would not be used if the optimal combination of outputs were produced.

INPUT	SHADOW PRICE	INPUT	SHADOW PRICE
Computer Services	+	Space	
		Instructional	0
Counseling	+	Laboratory	+
		Office	0
Dean of Faculties	+		
Dean of Graduate School	+	Student Services	0
		(All Types)	
Dean, Arts and Sciences	+		
College		Telephone & Telegraph	0
Dean, Applied Sciences	0	Testing	0
and Technology College			
		Biology Service*	
Dean, Education College	0	Hours—100**	+
		200	+
Dean, Business College	+	300	0
		400	0
Dean, Fine Arts College	0		
		Chemistry Service	
Mail and Postage	0	Hours—100	+
		200	+
News and Publications	0	300	0
		400	0
Personnel			
Faculty (All Types)	0	Economics Service	
Non-Faculty (All Types)	0	Hours—100	+
		200	+
Placement	+	300	+
		400	+

INPUT	SHADOW PRICE	INPUT	SHADOW PRICE
English Service		Political Science Service	
Hours—100	0	Hours—100	+
200	0	200	+
300	0	300	+
400	0	400	+
Foreign Language Service		Psychology Service	
Hours—100	+	Hours—100	0
200	0	200	0
300	0	300	0
400	0	400	0
Geography-Geology Service		Sociology-Anthropology Service	
Hours—100	+	Hours—100	+
200	+	200	+
300	+	300	+
400	+	400	+
History Service		Speech-Service	
Hours—100	+	Hours—100	+
200	+	200	0
300	+	300	0
400	+	400	0
Library Science Service		Agriculture Service	
Hours—100	+	Hours—100	0
		200	0
Mathematics Service		300	0
Hours—100	+		
200	+	Home Economics Service	
300	+	Hours—100	0
400	+	200	0
		300	0
Philosophy Service		400	0
Hours—100	+		
200	+	Industrial Technology Service	
300	+	Hours—100	0
		200	0
Physics Service		300	0
Hours—100	+	400	0
200	+		
300	+	Health and Physical Education	
400	+	(Men's) Service	
		Hours—100	0
		200	0
		300	0
		400	0

Health and Physical Education (Women's) Service		Special Education Service	
Hours—100	0	Hours—100	0
200	0	200	0
300	0	300	0
400	0	400	0
Education Service		Art Service	
Hours—100	0	Hours—100	0
200	0	200	0
300	0	300	0
400	0	400	0
Educational Administration Service Hours		Music Service	
—300	0	Hours—100	0
400	0	200	0
		300	0
		400	0

* Service courses are those courses offered by a given department which are taken by students in other departments for any reason. If a given department services another department whose output contracts in the optimal solution, then the first department's service offerings are also likely to contract.

** The appellation "100" refers to a course numbered 100-199; "200" refers to a course numbered 200-299, etc. 100 level courses are open to all students and are beginning courses. 200 level courses are open only to junior and senior students. 300 level courses are open only to students with junior, senior, or graduate standing. 400 level courses are open only to graduate students.

NOTES

1. For purposes of brevity, the adjective "public" will hereinafter be omitted when reference is made to the university. The nature of the model and its society-wide viewpoint make the model more applicable to a public university than to a private university.

2. The problem is not trivial. *The Chronical of Higher Education* [9] reported that direct state governmental appropriations to public universities in the United States would exceed seven billion dollars in the academic year 1971–72.

3. This view of the university is obviously market-oriented and ignores research and public service activities. Such resources should ordinarily be excluded from the total resource constraint confronting the university prior to the application of the model described here. The interested reader is referred to [16] for an animated discussion of the outputs of higher education.

4. It is undoubtedly true that higher education causes external economies and diseconomies. The argument made here, however, is that: (1) the external economies are smaller than originally thought or even nonexistent [13]; and, (2) the external diseconomies associated with higher education (for example, the shopworn example of the university-educated accountant whose education introduced him to sophisticated ways to cheat on his income tax) are significant and have been largely ignored. Hence, this study assumes that the net value to society of higher education externalities is zero. The model is sufficiently general, however, to permit the inclusion of external economies and diseconomies if their precise magnitude can be ascertained.

5. This project looks upon higher education expenditures as an investment which may yield future returns. It is possible that some individuals might regard a proportion of such expenditures as consumption expenditures which yield pleasure and cultural benefits at the very time the expenditures are made. Such expenditures are not an investment cost and must be treated like any other consumption expenditure (for example, the purchase of a pizza). On the other hand, Blaug [7] has pointed out that many college students experience great disutility in the higher education process. High collegiate drop-out rates and low class attendance are impressionistic evidence in support of the disutility argument. It can be argued that when aggregates of students are considered (as in this study), consumption benefits may well sum to zero.

The question is not unimportant empirically. Assume that students regard one-quarter of their expenditures on higher education as consumption expenditures. This reduces the investment cost of their education by 25 per cent. Then, for example, the 9 per cent rate of return on investment which Becker [5] computed rises to over 14 per cent.

The easiest way to avoid the problem is to assume that consumption benefits sum to zero when large numbers of students are considered. That approach has been taken in this study. However, it should be noted that when consumption expenditures actually are nonzero, but do constitute a given proportion of total expenditures made in each academic area, the same results are generated by this model as are generated in the case where consumption expenditures are assumed to be zero in net terms.

6. The impact of this assumption is to involve the university in ameliorating surpluses and shortages of university-trained personnel when the benefit to cost ratio attached to such activity so dictates.

7. Hansen and Weisbrod [13] have provided a discussion of the above issues which is at once thorough and not lacking in rigor, but also is written with great clarity. An important bibliographic summary of the mountainous economics of education literature which includes over 1300 items may be found in Hüfner [14].

8. The dual problem may be conceptually formulated as follows:

$$\text{Minimize:} \quad \theta = K_1V_1 + K_2V_2 + \ldots + K_mV_m$$

$$\text{Subject to:} \quad a_{11}V_1 + a_{21}V_2 + \ldots + a_{m1}V_m \geq P_1$$

$$a_{12}V_1 + a_{22}V_2 + \ldots + a_{m2}V_m \geq P_2$$

$$\cdot \quad \cdot \quad \cdot \quad \cdot \quad \cdot$$

$$\cdot \quad \cdot \quad \cdot \quad \cdot \quad \cdot$$

$$\cdot \quad \cdot \quad \cdot \quad \cdot \quad \cdot$$

$$a_{1n}V_1 + a_{2n}V_2 + \ldots + a_{mn}V_m \geq P_n$$

$$\text{where } V_j = \text{shadow price of input } j$$

9. Becker [6] estimated that 12 per cent of the income differential between college and high school graduates was attributable to factors such as ability and motivation. Denison [11] has suggested that 40 per cent of the differential is due to such factors. Hansen and Weisbrod [13] argue for the 25 per cent adjustment.

10. See Weisbrod and Karpoff [22].

11. The probability of the death of a given graduate was taken from U.S. Department of Health, Education and Welfare [20]; labor force participation rates of Illinois State University graduates were obtained from the Illinois State University Placement Bureau.

12. A study conducted by Larsen [15] at Illinois State University indicated that the typical graduate of a "four year" baccalaureate degree program required almost four and one-half years of university attendance to attain that degree.

13. Schultz [18] must be given the lion's share of the credit for pointing out that foregone incomes must be considered to be a cost.

14. Long-run constraints are defined here as those constraints which need not be satisfied in a given year, but which must be satisfied over a space of several years. For example, an external constraint imposed on Illinois State University by the Illinois Board of Higher Education calls for a 10 per cent reduction in Illinois State's production of teachers over a space of three years. This constraint actually need not be satisfied in any except the third year.

15. Three different types of space were defined: instructional, office, and laboratory.

16. See, for example, Baumol [4] and substantive comments concerning his paper in the December, 1969, and March 1970, issues of the *American Economic Review.*

17. Linear programming is hardly a new technique to economists. Nevertheless, it has seldom been applied to problems of resource and manpower allocation inside universities. Exceptions include Adelman [1], Bowles [8], DeWoolf [12], and Plessner, Fox, and Sanyal [17].

18. It was necessary to use national data because the Placement Bureau at Illinois State University did not possess sufficiently complete age-earnings profiles on Illinois State graduates.

19. The actual numeric values of the optimal solution are of little interest to anyone not familiar with Illinois State University and (in any case) have no meaning unless accompanied by comprehensive information about the current mixture of outputs and inputs they would replace. Further the reproduction of such comprehensive information might seriously compromise the confidential nature of the study without achieving any corresponding gain in descriptive power.

REFERENCES

1. Adelman, I. "A Linear Programming Model of Educational Planning: A Case Study of Argentina," in I. Adelman and E. Thorbecke (eds.), *The Theory and Design of Economic Development* (Baltimore: The Johns Hopkins Press, 1966), Chapter 14.

2. *American Science Manpower,* 1969. (Washington, D.C.: U.S. Government Printing Office, 1970).

3. *Annual Survey of Recruiting Practices and Results* (Chicago: Midwest College Placement Association, 1970).

4. Baumol, William. "On the Social Rate of Discount," *American Economic Review,* Vol. 58 (September, 1968), pp. 788–802.

5. Becker, Gary. *Human Capital* (Princeton: Princeton University Press, 1964).

6. Becker, Gary. "Underinvestment in College Education?," *American Economic Review,* Vol. 50 (May, 1960), pp. 346–54.

7. Blaug, Mark. "The Rate of Return on Investment in Education in Great Britain," *The Manchester School,* Vol. 33 (September, 1965), pp. 205–51.

8. Bowles, Samuel. "A Planning Model for the Efficient Allocation of Resources in Education," Paper presented at the 1965 Meetings of the Econometric Society, New York.

9. "State Funds For Colleges Seen Topping $7.5 Billion," *The Chronicle of Higher Education* (October 4, 1971), p. 8.

10. Colberg, Marshall, and Windham, Douglas. "Age-Income Profiles and Invidious Comparisons," *Mississippi Valley Review of Business and Economics,* Vol. 6 (Winter, 1970), pp. 28–40.

11. Denison, Edward F. *The Sources of Economic Growth.* (Washington, D.C.: Committee for Economic Development, 1962).

12. DeWoolf, P. "Models for Manpower and Educational Planning," Paper Presented at the 1965 Meetings of the Allied Social Science Association, New York.

13. Hansen, W. Lee, and Weisbrod, Burton A. *Benefits, Costs and Finance of Public Higher Education* (Chicago: Markham Publishing Company, 1969).

14. Hüfner, Klaus. "Economics of Higher Education and Educational Planning—A Bibliography," *Socio-Economic Planning Sciences,* Vol. 2 (1968), pp. 25–101.

15. Larsen, Arthur H. *Who Graduates?* (Normal, Illinois: Illinois State University, 1971).

16. Lawrence, Ben, Weatherby, George, and Patterson, Virginia W. (eds.). *The Outputs of Higher Education: Their Identification, Measurement, and Evaluation* (Boulder, Colorado: Western Interstate Commission for Higher Education, 1970).

17. Plessner, Yakir, Fox, Karl A., and Sanyal, Bikas C. "On the Allocation of Resources in a University Department," *Metroeconomica,* Vol. 20 (September-December, 1968), pp. 256–71.

18. Schultz, Theodore. "Capital Formation by Education," *Journal of Political Economy,* Vol. 68 (December, 1960), pp. 571–83.

19. Staff of the Board of Higher Education of the State of Illinois. *Memorandum to University Presidents and Systems Heads, November 30, 1971.*

20. United States Department of Health, Education, and Welfare, "United States Life Tables, 1959–1961," *Public Health Service, No. 1252, Vol. 1.* (Washington, D.C.: United States Government Printing Office, 1964).

21. Vaizey, John. *The Economics of Education.* (New York: The Free Press of Glencoe, 1962).
22. Weisbrod, Burton A., and Karpoff, Peter A. "Monetary Returns to College Education," *Review of Economics and Statistics,* Vol. 50 (November, 1968), pp. 491–97.

Comments on "On the Allocation of Resources and the Training of Manpower in a University"

Stephen Resnick*

I found this to be an interesting application of linear programming to an important administrative problem of how to allocate resources efficiently within the university. Certainly nowadays with cutback in budgets, decreased enrollments for some schools, and in general hard times for some higher education institutions, the application of such a model can provide some needed quantitative answers to where scarce resources should be allocated and where they should not.

One would think that the results of this model would be of interest to university administrators. Implementation of the program's results may, however, be a different story. Here the suggestion that a department be cut back, or at least not be allowed to expand, might involve various types of political battles within the university, assuming that the affected department fights for its academic life. For example, Note 19 states that:

> actual numerical values or the optimal solution are of little interest to anyone not familiar with Illinois State University...further, the reproduction of such comprehensive information might seriously compromise the confidential nature of the study....

Now, if I were in the Education Department, I would be more than

*Professor of Economics, University of Massachusetts. The author was an Associate Professor of Economics at the City College of the City University of New York when he delivered these comments.

slightly interested in such information given that the solution of the program indicates that this department be cut. In fact, my initial reaction in reading Table *I*, where the results are given, was to check to see if Economics had a plus or negative sign, indicating respectively expansion or contraction. Being satisfied with the plus sign, I could then examine the model's assumptions with some peace of mind.

At this point, I would like to raise some questions concerning the paper.

(1) It is not clear to me why the model is more applicable to a public rather than a private university. Perhaps there are different objective functions involved here, but that in itself would be an interesting topic for discussion.

(2) The author spends some time discussing assumptions underlying the specified objective functions and makes a strong case for the model. However, the discussion of education causing external economies and diseconomies has a curious footnote (see Note 4). This note ends with the statement that: "... .the model is sufficiently general, however, to permit the inclusion of external economies and diseconomies if their precise magnitude can be ascertained." This does not help us very much. The problem is the proper identification and magnitude of these economies, not so much that the model is capable of incorporating them.

(3) I am not sure what are all the implications of Assumption *3* of *The Underlying Assumptions*. I wonder how much of an individual's income over time can be attributed to education? Also, are there any other objectives that a university might or should have besides that future income of its students? And, what are the relationships between the objectives of a university and society? Should the university be, and, in fact, is it just a passive agent accepting market signals like income?

(4) The model takes into account the fact that outputs of each department depend upon inputs from other departments. But there is a qualitative as well as quantitative relationship here that presumably adds up to what historically we consider a university to be—a very difficult animal to quantify.

In general, what are the educational and intellectual complementarities among fields in a university and within a department? This problem is too important to be left to the computer, but the computer may force us to face it.

(5) Finally, I found this paper to be a good catalyst in raising several questions in my mind about a university that I had not thought about in some time.

   (a) How can the university increase the productivity of its resources? Do we have a measure of productivity? And, are there simultaneous relationships among inputs?

   (b) How important is the quality of these resources in affecting output, e.g., the quality of offices, classrooms, faculty member, food, so forth?

   (c) There may be a need for more of a systems approach to measure educational costs and benefits, but this need carries with it the danger of being mystified by the technique, and forgetting to ask continuously the basic questions of what we are doing within a university and why are we doing it.

8

The New Brain Drain from Developing Countries: International Costs and Benefits, 1960–72

Edwin P. Reubens*

"...at the new medical school in Chiengmai, Thailand, virtually the whole of the first graduating class chartered an airplane and flew off to the United States."

This monitory tale—recounted by Dr. Thomas Dublin[1] and sounding apocryphal, but substantially confirmed by authorities interviewed recently in Bangkok—expresses the essence of the new "brain drain." It is a complex and troublesome form of older migratory movements, responding with greater mobility than ever before to differential levels of welfare and different rates of development in various regions of the world.

From the end of the 1950's to the mid-1960's, public concern was focussed on the migration of certain professional personnel —notably scientists and engineers, physicians, and other medical personnel—from Great Britain and some other European nations to the magnetic nations of North America. After 1967, this kind of drain subsided, and the return flow rose.

From the mid-1960's, attention and alarm turned to the new kind of drain whose trend was rising. This was the migration of professionals and skilled workers from the less developed and de-

*The author is Professor of Economics at the City College of New York, specializing in economic development and human capital. He has served as consultant to the U.S. Agency for International Development and to the United Nations, at headquarters and in areas of Europe, Asia, Africa and the Caribbean, and as an adviser to governments in several of these areas.

veloping countries to the already advanced nations; and especially to the U.S. after 1965 (responding to successive revisions and liberalizations of the immigration regulations). Controversy over this "drain" was further heated up—rather paradoxically—by the restrictions which during the 1960's the British imposed on immigration there, as well as by the education-repayment charge which the Soviet Union in Summer 1972 imposed on would-be emigrants from that nation.

The swelling flow of qualified personnel from the underdeveloped regions is commonly supposed to enrich the already prosperous nations at the expense of the lagging ones, and thereby to widen the lag. Most of the official reports and popular discussions have assumed—rather than demonstrated—that the *gross* outflows of personnel were almost all *net* outflows; and that all net outflows were a significant *net loss* to all the nations of emigration; and that all the net inflows were a significant *net gain* to all the receiving nations; and that all the migrating individuals and families were rejecting positions of *high social utility at home* for the sake of selfish personal gain abroad. Thus the brain drain from the developing countries, viewed in nationalistic terms, has come to be denounced in Third World circles as "bourgeois materialism" as well as "exploitation by the rich countries," also called "reverse lend-lease," "negative foreign assistance," and "neo-colonialism."

Meanwhile, technical economic analyses were evolving in the opposite direction, toward a very different model, conceived in "internationalist" terms on a base of static allocation theory. Neoclassical economists—notably Harry Johnson, H. D. Grubel and A. D. Scott, Hla Myint, E. J. Mishan,[2] among others—devised certain applications of human-capital theory, which in turn is derived from marginal productivity analysis under conditions of perfect markets. These economists asserted that professional migration was simply the labor market at work on the international scene. As professionals moved to the locations which could offer them the highest compensation (reflecting, it was assumed, the highest level of real productivity of such professionals), benefit was maximized not only for the individual migrants (in the form of higher net incomes) and for the country of immigration (by raising its productivity), but also for the country of emigration (which obtained a vent for surplus labor, receipt of remittances, eventual return of some more skilled and experienced personnel, as well as some eventual trading benefits). Climaxing this list of Panglossian cold comforts was the maximization of benefit for the whole "world-economy," via optimal allocation of world labor, and promotion of the world's scientific and technological knowledge.

While the Third World-ers charge that the Brain Drain is big and bad; and the neo-classicals declare that, whether big or small, it is ultimately good; yet a third model has appeared: asserting that this movement of "brains" is seldom a "drain" at all, but rather is, in most countries, simply an "overflow" (in George Baldwin's term).[3] This is said to be the case wherever migrants were "surplus personnel"—i.e., a situation where their marginal productivity at home was strictly zero (if not actually negative). Accordingly the opportunity cost of such migrants is said to be nil.

Facing these problems of migration, the responsible public official, caught between the extremes of politics and economics, looks to the scholars to find viable middle grounds. In turn, for the scholars to resolve those prolonged and inconclusive debates, data must replace assumptions, history must constrain abstract speculations, and principles of economic development must be applied to clarify the benefits and costs of international migration.

Fortunately for this undertaking, national migration statistics and occupational data have been greatly improved during the last few years; and a number of country studies have been made in some depth.[4]

In the following pages, first we sketch the features of an appropriate Benefit/Cost model. Then we evaluate the professional immigration into the most concerned countries of the developed group. Then we explore the case of emigration from India, and compare it with divergent types of other developing countries. The concluding section considers alternative policies for national and international action.

I. *An Appropriate Benefit/Cost Model*

The concepts of benefit/cost analysis provide a general

framework for examining and measuring the effects of migration.

Our first step is to define the entities whose benefits and costs will be measured—that is, whether to focus on the individuals directly concerned, or on their national state, or on an "international economy." In the present study we adopt predominantly a national-economy approach.

This is not to deny the personal-welfare considerations which occupy much of the brain-drain literature. But we give them small emphasis in comparison with the possible macro-economic effects of migration on national production and employment and consumption. Conversely, an internationalist pattern of benefits and costs depends upon the diverse situations of the several countries.

The next step is to select the relevant features of each economy involved in emigration and immigration. A full model would incorporate six such variables: (a) on the labor supply side: the gross and net figures on the migrant flow or stock as a percentage of the national flow or stock of the occupations in question; (b) on the labor demand side: ratios of net professional migration to vacancies or unemployment in those occupations, taking account of grade and salary differentials; (c) effects upon the national product, total employment, and their growth; (d) effects upon the national capital and its utilization; (e) indirect effects ("externalities"), especially upon relative factor prices, the overall price level, and the balance of international payments; (f) distributional effects upon the welfare of individuals and groups.

The above features (c)–(f), dealing with the whole economy, are far more difficult to measure than (a) and (b) which deal with occupational supplies and demands. Fortunately for the discussion of the countries which receive professional immigration, it will be shown that the net inflow is relatively quite small. Accordingly the effects will be so small that it is not necessary to undertake measuring all of (c)–(f) in order to derive guidelines for policy—although some of these features, e.g., the capital value embodied in immigrants, will be estimated as needed.

As regards the developing countries and the economic effects of emigration upon them, all of the dynamic considerations are of the essence. Nevertheless, here the investigation is reduced in part because in some countries the emigrating professionals are surplus at home and accordingly cause little or no dislocation or production loss—although the transfer of embodied capital is worth computing. On the other hand, other developing countries suffer appreciable damage from every professional departure, such that the full range of economic effects should be estimated—unless the number of emigrating persons is actually small.

In the final consolidation of the brain-losing with the brain-gaining cases, the possibility arises that professional migration may bring only a relatively small gain to the receiving countries, while imposing a relatively large loss upon some source countries, and bringing a small loss, or actual net gain, to some other source countries. In short, if the international brain drain could be evaluated as to its net effects upon worldwide welfare in the "internationalist" sense, it might prove to be anything from a "negative sum game" through a possible "zero sum" to perhaps a positive net balance!

Within the foregoing broad outline of a benefit/cost model, we will give little attention to private returns, and instead concentrate on the migration of professionals in terms of net social marginal product *(SMP)* from this input compared to the *SMP* of substitutable inputs.

In accordance with these principles, we exclude from our calculations the role of exceptional individuals, the "key men" much stressed in the lterature, who are credited with large and sometimes extraordinary contributions. The occurrence of such special persons, while undeniable, is variable and unpredictable. They are usually impossible to identify *a priori;* and could be kept at home only by some prohibition on all emigration. Furthermore, they are by definition unique and irreplaceable; and their performance may be tied to a singular context; such that their value cannot be discussed in terms of substitutable inputs.

Another important issue to which we apply the principle of substitutable inputs generating net social marginal product is the monetary evaluation of an immigrant. In the existing literature it has become common practice to take "lifetime earnings" as the measure of an immigrant's economic contribution (and as the measure of the losses imposed upon the country he left). But this practice has not learned the lesson of social rate-of-return analysis in modern human-capital theory, which focusses on the *differentials* in output attributable to *incremental* education, i.e., the additional output produced by a professional man over what would have been produced on the average if his education had halted at the pre-professional stage. As these differentials amount to only between 20% and 30% of the absolute earnings of a professional man in the U.S.A.,[5] the present value of a qualified immigrant should be reduced by some three-fourths from certain figures widely circulated today.

Furthermore, it becomes apparent that the net social benefit from immigration is not to be found on the output or earnings side, since the contribution of an immigrant is not essentially different from the contribution of a trainable and substitutable native person, when both are functioning in the same economy in the same line of work. Clearly the benefit is to be found on the cost-of-training side: the saving of educational expenditure and apprenticeship provisions when both the direct costs of schooling and the foregone earnings of a student or trainee were incurred abroad. In other words, the real social gain from immigration is the opportunity cost: the avoided costs of educating and training another native to professional qualifications.

This formulation, for the real social value of the immigration of professionals, falls in the middle of a wide range of possible measures, each of which has its advocates. These measures include: (1) the cost of producing the migrant in his home country, (2) the cost of producing an equivalent in the country of immigration, (3) the value of his foregone (marginal) output in his home country, and (4) the value of his (marginal) contribution to output in the country of immigration. While we take the outputs as *marginal* in the economy of the two countries, we take the training costs as *average*—partly because the volumes of migration are usually large enough to represent the output of one or more whole schools, and partly because educational data generally give average but not marginal costs.

Of these four measures, the lowest will often be #3, as it can fall all the way to nothing when trained personnel has been over-produced, shows significant unemployment, and has a marginal productivity of zero. The highest measure will ordinarily be #4; however, in this paper we treat that measure of contribution as irrelevant, on the ground that the immigrant ordinarily contributes to output neither more nor less than a native who was trained—or could be trained—to the same competence. The immigrant's contribution is therefore to be found specifically in the training cost which he saves the country of immigration. This saving, #2, is ordinarily larger than #1, the training cost at home; it is often very much larger, as shown in section *IV* below.

Another important implication of the SMP approach bears on foreign students who do not return home, and the vexed question of whether they should be included in total brain drain. According to our model, they should be excluded. Foreign students —especially those from Asia—who receive their professional training in an advanced nation are mostly carried at *that nation's expense* (taking account of official grants, academic fellowships, and students' part-time earnings).[6] Those who subsequently do not return home should not be considered "brain drain"; just as they are not "brain gain" to the receiving economy.

II. *LDC Professionals in MDC Economies*

Table *1* presents the gross-inflow record of professionals from less developed countries (LDC) who have come to practice their professions in more developed countries (MDC). The data have been extracted and assembled from the immigration statistics of United Kingdom, Canada and the U.S.A.—the three nations which receive the vast majority of these migrants.

The tabulation—together with less specific data for earlier years—shows that in the U.K. the inflow was at a peak early in the 1960's and has subsequently been sharply reduced, largely by restrictive legislation and administration. In the case of Canada, which showed a rising trend, restraints were imposed after 1966. The U.S.A. has always been the largest recipient; and after the regulations were liberalized in 1965, the reported "admissions" zoomed far beyond the other receiving countries. The three-country total doubled from the early part to the latter part of the

1960's, and rose by another 30 per cent to the 1971–1972 level, but was cut back in 1973.

It should be noted that "admissions" to permanent residence in some countries include foreign students converting to permanent residence status (instead of returning home) as well as foreigners arriving with professional qualifications. This has long been the practice in the U.S. statistics, and in Canada since 1967. In the U.S. the proportion of converting students in the totals has fluctuated over recent years, reaching a peak of over 27 per cent in 1967, and now stands at about 20 per cent.

Another item is also to be deducted from the gross inflows in order to arrive at the "net foreign contribution of immigration." This is the annual outflow of foreign-born professionals who, having arrived some time earlier, leave for home or other countries, in magnitudes discussed below under each MDC country.

TABLE 1

GROSS IMMIGRATION OF PROFESSIONAL AND TECHNICAL
PERSONNEL FROM LESS DEVELOPED COUNTRIES INTO
THE UNITED STATES, CANADA AND UNITED KINGDOM
1962-1972

Year	United States	Canada	United Kingdom	3-country sum
1962	9,024	1,472		
1963	11,029	1,642	4,600	17,271
1964	11,418	1,991	—	
1965	11,001	3,826	3,230	18,057
1966	13,986	4,891	—	
1967	23,361	4,812	2,900	31,073
1968	28,511	4,683	2,420	35,614
1969	27,536	5,447	1,720	34,703
1970	33,796	4,636	1,000	39,432
1971	38,647	4,815	1,220	44,682
1972	39,106			

Note: Coverage of "Professional and technical personnel" is based on "Professional, technical, and kindred workers" in the usage of the United States Immigration and Naturalization Service, *Annual*

Reports, Table 8; data for Canada are taken from the closest corresponding occupational categories as reported by Department of
Manpower and Immigration, annual *Immigration Statistics,* Table 11,
categories 2–48 inclusive; data for United Kingdom derived from
special tables in E. J. B. Rose, *et. al., Colour and Citizenship,* pp. 83,
86, for the period 1962–1966, and from Home Office,
Commonwealth Immigrants Statistics, annual reports for period
1967–71, Table 9 covering arrivals of holders of "Category B vouchers." Listing of persons by occupation is generally based on the
immigrant's own declaration. U.S.A. data refer to fiscal years (ending 30 June); other countries are in calendar years.

A. *United Kingdom*

Starting with Britain and the inflow/stock ratio, we find that
gross immigration of LDC professionals at the British peak rates of
the early 1960's amounted to a tiny annual increment to that
country's aggregate stock of professionals. It was about one-fifth of
one per cent a year at that time and became less at the low inflow
rates prevailing in 1970 and 1971 (about one-fourth of the peak
rates). Still lower ratios would emerge if we could move from gross
inflows to net inflows, by subtracting return flows; not much is
known on this matter, but scattered evidence suggests substantial
return rates: they are known to amount, in the case of foreign doctors in Britain, to some 40–60 per cent of the current gross inflow
of such doctors, and the average return rates are perhaps 25–30
per cent annually for the whole professional category.

For certain particular professions, the LDC inflow was more substantial. The major instance is the medical profession, where gross
immigration of LDC doctors in the early 1960's added about 3 per
cent a year to the country's stock. However, by the early 1970's the
annual increment had fallen to three-fourths of 1 per cent. Allowance for return flows would bring the net contribution down to
about half of the foregoing ratios for doctors.[7]

Turning to the stock/stock ratio—which measures the accumulation of the net inflows over the years—we find that the stock of
LDC professionals in Britain was 3.2 per cent of the aggregate professional stock in 1966, according to the sample census in that year.

In view of subsequent trends, this ratio is certainly no higher today, probably lower. In some particular professions, however, the LDC ratios in 1966 were at levels far above the average: e.g., among scientists and engineers, 4.1 per cent; among nurses, 6–9 per cent (although earlier estimates ran as high as 20 or 25 per cent). Among doctors in total, the LDC ratio reached almost 15 per cent; and in certain lower grades of doctor employment, which relied heavily upon foreign-born staff, the LDC share was as high as 63 per cent. All these percentages, however, must be reduced sharply to allow for professional training in Britain rather than abroad: thus reducing the LDC ratio among doctors by two-fifths, and by more for nurses, but by less for scientists and engineers.

Proceeding beyond these numerical ratios to the functional significance of the LDC professionals in the British economy, we consider their contributions to the British labor market. For the professional category as a whole there seems to be little need for the immigrants in the sense of unfillable vacancies. In fact, reported unemployment rates for recent university graduates have been in the range of 4–6 per cent. Surveys by the Department of Trade and Industry have found that many graduates have been hired to fill vacancies among the technicians and technical supporting staff, where real shortages may in fact exist. A recently initiated series by the Department of Employment indicates that among males in professional occupations as a group, the unemployed are about five times the number of vacancies: this suggests surplus, not shortage. The chief exception is in the female list, for the nursing profession, where the unemployed persons are only 20–30 per cent of the available notified vacancies, suggesting a real shortage of nurses.

The aggregate economic contribution of the LDC professionals to the British economy may be evaluated—in accordance with our model—at the time of their arrival in Britain: by estimating the direct costs of the British equivalent of the education and training brought in by these immigrants. The 1966 stock of LDC professionals in Britain—a net accumulation which counts those who obtained their qualifications in Britain as well as those who were trained abroad—had a cost value of embodied training perhaps worth as much as £ 360 million in very inclusive British terms and

1964 prices;[8] the cost value of actual training received abroad would be considerably less.

As for the flow aspect of the LDC brain gain, the annual gross inflow in 1970 and 1971—counting only new immigrants who had already qualified—was worth up to £ 15 million a year, in British prices adjusted to 1971 (again using very inclusive estimates of unit costs of education in Britain). This value of annual gross inflow, related to the current GNP of Britain, amounted to about .03 of 1 per cent thereof. Related to the British government's annual outlay for education at all levels, the aforesaid gross inflow amounted to about .6 of 1 per cent of that outlay. For the immigration flows in the early 1960's, when the inflows were much larger, and the real GNP and the real educational outlays were smaller, the foregoing ratios should be multiplied by about a factor of 5. For evaluating the inflows net of returns, the foregoing percentages should be reduced by about one-fourth.

B. *Canada*

As the Canadian census data published to date do not provide full detail on the national origins of all the professionals working in that country, we can make only a rough estimate of the stock of LDC professionals, blown up from the reported number of professionals of "Asiatic birthplace." This estimate suggests that LDC professionals were perhaps 1–2 per cent of the total professional stock in Canada in 1961.

For the stock in particular professions, we find that in 1967 LDC personnel accounted for a little over 2 per cent of Canada's total stock of engineers, 3 per cent of Canada's natural scientists, and about 2 per cent of her social scientists and of other scientifically-trained personnel.[9] A narrower coverage—to count only those immigrants who received their professional training abroad—would sharply reduce those percentages.

As for the flow rates, the gross inflow of LDC professionals, summarized over the ten years 1962–71—with no reduction for return outflows, or for retirements and deaths—came to just over 38,000 persons. These constituted a summary contribution of 6 per cent to the stock of 628,911 professionals in Canada at the beginning of this period. Accordingly, the average annual rate of gross inflow of LDC professionals was .6 of 1 per cent a year over the 1962–71 period. For the higher levels of inflow prevailing during 1966–71 sub-period, the annual ratio was .7 of 1 per cent of the enlarged stock. If return flows could be estimated and subtracted, also deducting student conversions since 1967, the net annual inflow would be at still lower rates.

Some particular professions, however, showed higher rates. Thus the gross inflow of LDC Engineers, Scientists and Doctors, during those ten years 1962–71, averaged annually between 1.1 and 1.6 per cent of the 1961 stock in these professions. On the other hand, lower than average rates of contribution to the stock appear for Teachers, Dentists, and unspecified Others; while Nurses (including Nurses-in-Training) were at the all-professional average of .6 of 1 per cent.

The trend of immigration for the individual professions also shows some variance from the trend for the total of professionals: there was a rather steady upward trend for Scientists, for Engineers, and for Others; there was a peak for Teachers and for Doctors in 1969, followed by a decline; and there was a peak for Nurses in 1966, followed by a very sharp decline. Increasing regulation of immigration, with a view to Canada's needs, played a large role in these trends.

C. *United States of America*

The magnitude of the professional immigration from developing countries into the United States has increased strongly during the past decade. Our concern here is its relative importance.

For the 1962–66 period, the average annual gross number (11,300) of LDC professionals "admitted" to the United States as residents works out to one-seventh of 1 per cent of the 1960 stock of professionals in this country (7.5 million persons); and less against the 1965 stock. At the much higher rates of inflow during 1967–69 (averaging 26,500 a year), taken against the then current stock (11.4 million in 1970), the annual ratio was about one-fourth of 1 per cent a year. When the inflow rate soared again after 1969 (to a level of about 39,000 a year in 1971 and 1972) the annual flow/stock ratio attained one-third of 1 per cent. Ten years of this rate of gross admissions—making no deductions for return flows of immigrants, nor for foreign students already in the United States converting to permanent residents—would add 3.33 per cent to the 1970 stock.

Our calculation of the relevant student conversions[10] finds that they amount to about 20 per cent of the reported annual gross immigration of professionals from LDC countries during the early 1970's. Our estimate of return flows comes to at least 30 per cent of the gross inflows.[11] Combining these two deductions, the above projected PTK inflow for ten years would be reduced from a 3.33 per cent gross increment to the 1970 stock, to about 1.66 per cent increment, counting only LDC immigrants arriving with professional qualifications and deducting all professionally qualified persons returning home to LDC countries.

Considering next the stock/stock ratio, we must await publication of the 1970 census for a complete picture of the net accumulations since the 1960 census. Meanwhile we have found that among scientists in the United States in 1966, LDC personnel amounted to just over 2 per cent of the stock; and in 1970 some 3 per cent of that stock.[12] Much the same percentages seem to hold for LDC engineers in the United States, according to our estimates, although the OECD data are not so specific as for scientists. In the medical profession as a whole—that is, disregarding questions of distribution among grades, salaries, locations, etc.—the accumulated stock of physicians from developing countries was in December 1970 about 10 per cent of the total stock of physicians in the United States.[13] While the LDC stock figures are net of returnees, they should be reduced for student conversions in the United States to arrive at qualified immigrants from abroad.

The third personnel measurement, flow/flow, may be constructed for the United States by setting the annual gross immigration of LDC professionals against the annual graduations of professionals from U.S. schools. For 1962–66, the resulting overall ratio comes to less than 2 per cent, and reaches 3½ per cent for 1967–69. With the still higher inflows observed in 1971 and 1972, this ratio rises to about 5 per cent. If student conversions are removed, this recent ratio falls to 4 per cent; if return flows are likewise deducted, the net ratio drops to 2½ per cent in these recent years.

Much higher flow/flow ratios had already been shown earlier for particular professionals. During 1965–69, the LDC gross inflow was about 16 per cent of engineering graduates here, and about 7 per cent for scientists.[14] For the following years these percentages should be raised by about 60 per cent to reflect the large increments from gross LDC immigration in 1970, 1971, and 1972. For physicians the 1970 LDC gross inflow was about 20 per cent of newly licensed physicians;[15] in 1972 it was actually about 44 per cent! However, we must recall once more that all these percentages become much smaller if the stated gross numbers of "immigrants" are reduced by some 20 per cent for non-returning student conversions, and by an additional 30 per cent of the gross for annual returns of former immigrants.

We turn now from the numerical flow/flow proportions of the professional immigration, to their labor market contribution. It should be noted first that during most of the 1960's the unemployment rate of professionals in the United States was very low. Most of the time that rate stood barely above 1 per cent (even below 1 per cent for some sub-categories, such as engineers). Such low rates probably represent merely job changing, voluntary leisure, and the like. It is reported that "through much of the 1960's, new graduates could barely keep pace with job openings and in a number of fields there were manpower scarcities."[16] In these circumstances, the inflow of LDC professionals—adding at most one-fourth of 1 per cent a year to the existing stock in the United States, as already noted—surely contributed to relieve the shortages in a small degree without posing any painful competition with native professionals, at least until quite late in the 1960's. During the early 1970's, however, the picture changed markedly, due to governmental cutbacks in technical programs and also due to general economic recession. Unemployment of professionals rose to a peak of over 3 per cent in 1971 (but receded slightly in 1972)[17]—just as a flood of new graduates came pouring out of the schools, and also just as the immigrants came streaming out of the less developed countries. It is perhaps a classic cobweb-type response. Appreciable reaction may now be expected, as immigrant professionals compete with natives for employment.

Probably the most urgent need filled by LDC professionals in the United States, as in Britain, is medical service at the junior levels. The foreign physicians flow disproportionately into the lower ranks in hospitals and clinics (especially in the public hospitals of New York, London, and other major cities); they flow heavily into urban ghettos, into night shifts, ambulance calls, and some other functions and locations avoided by native American doctors (but the foreigners avoid rural communities even more than the American doctors do).[18] Estimating from AMA data, perhaps one-fifth to one-fourth of all the interns and residents in American medical institutions have come from LDC nations.[19] In one sense, the foreign-born doctors are "releasing" native-born doctors to pursue more pleasing or more rewarding careers. In another sense, the foreigners are "reducing the pressure" to expand United States medical school facilities more widely, to produce more doctors on the supposition that the enlarged supply might trickle into the less attractive functions. To be sure, the foreign doctors are suffering discriminatory treatment when they are shunted into the less attractive jobs; but they are expected to be satisfied with the compensation of salaries well above those in their home countries.

The aggregate economic contribution of the LDC professional immigrants into the United States may be estimated as proposed in section *II* above, in terms of the avoided costs of educating another native to professional qualifications. We look first at the situation in the mid-1960's. We have constructed a relevant estimate of costs, counting only direct educational costs at the professional level, but including net income foregone there.[20] Applying this estimate, namely $15,000 per professional, to the net inflow of LDC professionals during 1962–66, an average of not more than 7,000 per year,[21] we arrive at a total value (replacement cost) of $105 million per year. The significance of this figure may be assessed against U.S. educational outlays during the same period. Set against the total expenditures by all levels of government for all levels of education (about $31 billion per year), the $105 million estimated replacement cost would come to a little over 1/3 of 1 per cent. Set against total expenditures on higher education alone (both public and private and including much sponsored research and public services but excluding all income foregone), which averaged $11 billion per year, the annual replacement cost shows up as 1 per cent.

Another line of significance is to set the estimated replacement cost, or "brain gain," against U.S. "foreign aid." The latter amounted, according to OECD figures, to $3,540 million per year transmitted to developing countries from the United States over the same years 1962–66, counting only "official development assistance" net of loan repayments (and excluding private foreign investments and other private transfers). In this calculation the "brain gain" to the United States from developing countries during the years 1962–66 amounted to about 3 per cent of the official foreign aid during that period.

After 1966, however, the surge of immigration from LDC countries enlarged the indicated contribution to the United States economy to a 1971 figure 3.5 times the average annual gross flow in 1962–66. When this physical increase (assuming a constant ratio of net to gross flows) is combined with the price rise in educational unit costs, and is related to the increased aggregate outlays for higher education (in current prices), the foreign contribution —calculated on the same basis as yielded 1 per cent for 1962–66—works out to 2.0 per cent of these educational outlays nowadays.

Similar extrapolations may be made with regard to U.S. foreign aid (which in gross flow barely changed from 1965–66 to 1971–72, but declined somewhat in net amount as debt service has increased, while the distribution among countries has shifted away from some accustomed recipients, and in favor of Vietnam and other East Asian countries). Accordingly, the contribution of the "brain gain" moves up from the measured 3 per cent in the earlier period to some 17.4 per cent of the annual official net aid outflow. An offset against this large measured upward movement is the rise of U.S. private foreign investment in these countries since 1966—more than offsetting the decline in net official aid.

III. *Professional Migration from Developing Nations: the Case of India*

The migration from India is of particular importance: the numbers of professional migrants from India is the second largest among all countries (first place belongs to the Philippines); the efforts for rational economic planning have been strenuous in that country; and the impression is still widespread that India typifies less developed countries suffering from a severe shortage of skilled personnel. On the other hand, the very magnitude of the Indian population, its severe poverty, unemployment, and underemployment, as well as its cultural traditions, may limit the relevance of India's experience for other developing nations.

A. *The migration record for India, 1962–72*

The data for measuring the migration of skilled personnel from India come mostly from the receiving countries. Table 2 presents estimates of the annual gross migration of professionals from India into U.S.A., Canada, and the U.K., plus an allowance for movements to other countries.

During the first half of the 1960's, the U.K. was by far the largest single recipient. Thereafter, the movement into the United Kingdom was severely reduced to quite small numbers, but the U.S.A. immigration swelled to unprecedented volume, while the

TABLE 2

INDIA: GROSS EMIGRATION[1] of PTK[2], 1962-72[3]

	TO: U.S.A.[4]	Canada[5]	U.K.[6]	3-Country Sum	Estimated total for world
1962-66 total	2,604	1,967	13,440	18,011	22,500
annual average 1962-66	521	393	2,688	3,602	4,500
1967	2,474	1,213	1,600	5,287	6,600
1968	2,189	812	1,581	4,582	5,700
1969	2,889	1,383	1,066	5,338	6,700
1970	5,171	1,049	454	6,674	8,300
1971	7,543	867	381	8,791	11,000
1972	8,171	n.a.	n.a.	9,201[7]	11,500[7]

1. Emigration data by occupation are not available from official statistical records of India. The table utilizes the immigration records of the three chief receiving countries. The sum of these figures for each year has been enlarged by one-fourth, and rounded to nearest hundred, to represent estimated worldwide coverage (last column), based on country-distribution of Indian professionals abroad according to voluntary register (CSIR, *Technical Manpower*, January 1972).

The figures in the table are "gross" in that no deduction has been made for return flows to India.

2. The occupational coverage of "professional, technical and kindred workers" follows the usage of the immigration authorities of the U.S.A., which in recent years has received the preponderant number of Indian PTK emigrants; and incorporates the closest available usage of the Canadian and British authorities. The occupational classification follows the immigrants' own declarations.

3. The data for U.S.A. refer to fiscal years (12 months ending 30 June of each year); data of other countries are for calendar years.

4. U.S.A. data from Immigration and Naturalization Service (I.N.S.) *Annual Reports*, Table 8 "Immigrants admitted by country or region of birth and major occupation group."

5. Canada data from Department of Manpower and Immigration, *Immigration Statistics*, 1962–71. Figures refer to immigrants whose former residence was in India: somewhat fewer than those born in India.

6. U.K. figures are our estimates, based mainly on Home Office, *Commonwealth Immigration Statistics*, annual, representing Indians arriving in Britain on "Category B Vouchers."

7. Estimated from U.S. actual figure, plus projections of declining trend for Canada and for the United Kingdom.

Canadian figures fluctuated without much trend. The estimated total of all gross migration of professionals from India shows a strong upward trend, raising the totals in 1971 and 1972 to 2½ times the 1962–66 average.

Similar data are available for the migration of the sub-categories of engineers and of physicians and surgeons (these data, however, show some gaps and disparities which must be filled by estimation).[22] For Indian engineers, the apparent gross migration trend has been steadily and strongly upward: from 960 for the 1962–66 annual average, to about 4,600 in 1971. For Indian physicians and surgeons, the numbers have been smaller than for engineers, and the rise has been slower: from a total of about 800 a year to all countries on the average for 1962–66, the migration rose slowly during the second half of the 1960's, but thereafter surged into the U.S.A. such that the 1971 total to all countries was 1,200 and in 1972 was probably half again as large.

All of these figures on migration from India are subject to two major adjustments which sharply reduce the numbers and especially flatten their upward trend. The first of these adjustments is to eliminate student visa conversions, insofar as attention is to be focussed on immigrant professionals and to exclude those who acquire their qualifications after entering the host country. In the U.S.A., figures for 1969, as much as 60 per cent of the reported "immigration" of Indian professionals of all kinds was accounted for by conversions of student visas.[23] In other words, only 40 per cent of that reported immigration represents the arrival of qualified professionals.

Immigration of Indians into Canada is also subject to an adjustment for students since 1967. As specific data are lacking for the case of India, we have applied to the Canadian gross inflow data the U.S. ratios for Indian student conversions since 1967.

The other major adjustment of reported immigration figures is to move from the gross inflow to the net flow. Until the information on the net stock increment becomes available from the 1970 and 1971 censuses, the net flow for India can be estimated roughly from some indicators of return flow rates.[24] Based on these sources, it seems likely that during the 1960's about 40 per cent of the reported gross migration of PTKs from India has been offset by return flows, most of which are returns to the home country. This is considerably above the estimate of 25 per cent given by Charles Kidd[25] for return flows of PTKs from Latin American countries who had entered the U.S.A. on immigrant visas during 1961–65; but the difference seems reasonable in the light of expressed attitudes, and in the light of the manpower surplus and related conditions in India and problems of assimilation here.

Combining the foregoing two adjustments on reported gross migration of PTK's—elimination of student conversions in foreign countries, and allowance for return flows to the home country—results in estimated figures for net immigration of already qualified PTK's from India to all foreign countries as follows:

1962–66 average	2,520
1969	2,010
1972	3,300

These adjusted figures are far below the gross figures which are commonly used in discussions of the Brain Drain. Indeed, our adjusted figures might be hard to accept, were it not for the strong confirmation implicit in the Indian authorities' estimate of the professional stock abroad as of 1970: since that estimate may be interpreted as a probable rate of net annual accumulation of about 2,000 such professional immigrants a year during the 1960's. Secondly, they show a trend much weaker than is commonly supposed: from the 1962–66 period which was dominated by migration to the U.K., to the late 1960's dominated by flows to the U.S.A., the net figures actually declined, as about half of reported gross immigration into the U.S. is actually conversion of students who received their training in the U.S., as distinguished from arrivals of already qualified foreign personnel. The surge of immigration after 1969, mainly into the U.S.A., carried the net flows to new but lower peaks after making the two adjustments: the 1972 figure was 1.6 times the 1962–66 figure (instead of nearly three times as shown by the gross figures before adjustment).

B. *Relative importance of Indian emigration*

India today presents an example of the emigration of skilled personnel who are "surplus" in that economy. This situation emerged early in the 1960's, and intensified sharply after 1965.

The overt evidence of such surpluses is the record of unemployment among skilled personnel, as reported for April 1971 by the Council of Scientific and Industrial Research in New Delhi.[26] This study shows unemployment rates that are "high" by Western standards. The highest rates of unemployment in 1971 are found among Science and among Arts personnel, running from 13 per cent up to 24 per cent. Next come the fields of Commerce, Agriculture, and Engineering. The lowest rates of unemployment are found among the Medical and Veterinary personnel, in the range of 5–7 per cent. The total idleness for the fields listed here comes to well over half a million persons with higher education. As these figures refer to persons completely unemployed at the time of the census in April 1971, additional thousands are presumed to have been "sub-employed"—i.e., employed in less than full-time work, or employed in occupations below their highest skill. It was found that nearly one-third of the unemployed persons had been in this situation for over two years.

The limited data available for earlier years suggests a strong rise in unemployment among professionals since 1961. Scientists and Engineers show the biggest jump from 1961 to 1971. The trend for Medical personnel, however, went in the opposite direction.

If we measure the stock of PTK as percentage of the total non-agricultural labor force,[27] and take account of different groups of countries, India with 6.3 per cent in 1961 (the date of the latest available general census) shows up as about average for LDC countries as a simple group. However, that percentage is appreciably above average considering India's low level of output per capita within the group.

While India thus appears to have had a relatively good supply of professionals back in 1961, the rapid expansion of India's educational output during the 1960's certainly pushed her stock further ahead. The number of physicians rose by 33 per cent from 1962 to 1966. The number of admissions into engineering schools during the second half of the 1960's was actually five times that of the second half of the 1950's. Meanwhile the economy grew more slowly: by about 3.4 per cent a year during the 1960's. It is no wonder that in many professional fields surpluses emerged and swelled. These effects were particularly marked in the field of engineering.[28]

It would take us too far afield to explore in detail the social causes of excessive educational expansion in India. Instead, we cite the conclusions of the intensive study by Blaug, Layard and Woodhall a few years ago;[29]

> The causes of educated unemployment in India run deep in the functioning of Indian labour markets, the hiring practices of the government, the institution of the joint family, and the personal values of educated Indians. The basic thread, however, is the difficulty of moving from a stage where education is scarce and yields high returns to a stage where education is widely diffused and no longer commands financial privilege. The high returns of the past produce an upsurge in the demand for education, and expansion acquires a momentum which cannot easily be resisted when altered circumstances require a change of

policy. . . .The process has probably gone further in India than anywhere else, but India is the mirror in which the developing countries of Africa and Asia can see the problem they will be facing in the decade of the 1970s.

It remains only to add that the advanced nations of the Western world also face this problem of excessive education, and Japan too may soon confront it. But the advanced nations, with high output per capita, can afford to support this burden, whether in the form of rising "credentialism" for employment or in the form of "education as consumption." The less developed nations, however, with small resources per capita, cannot manage to "put everything first."

C. *Cost/benefit evaluation of Indian migration*

In the case of professionals emigrating from India in recent years, the opportunity cost may be taken as zero, because the marginal product of surplus personnel is nil, and the annual emigration runs far below the persistent stock of unemployed professionals. This is the case in every country like India where the bottleneck on output is capital shortage or some other factor or condition rather than shortage of technical personnel.

There remains, however, a definite investment loss from emigration, measurable as the total outlays properly attributable to the emigrant's preparation. This gross cost, which is not ordinarily compensated by the receiving country (as is done for exported goods or provided services), may be partly offset by remittances sent home by the emigrant, or capital brought by him on his return home, but these transfers are not accurately known in most countries, and are usually believed to be small in India in relation to the preparation outlays. However, newly available data—from the UNITAR study of foreign students in the U.S., and broadly confirmed by the "longitudinal study" of Canada's immigrants now under way in the Department of Immigration—suggest that on the average an Indian professional during his stay in the U.S. sends home to India at least $2,500. This amount comes to more than the direct educational costs of preparing such a professional in India, or at least 60 per cent of the more inclusive measure of preparation as calculated below.

Also to be credited is the value of additional skills brought home by returning emigrants. But this is presumed to be accounted for by using net emigration figures in the aggregate cost calculation.

As the estimation of professional schooling costs in India is a large task, we begin with the engineering profession, for which two careful studies are available;[30] and we estimate with and without imputed earnings foregone. For degree engineers in India, we have figures as of 1960 and 1965 for the several levels at issue. According to Gounden's careful study for 1960, counting the reported costs for all levels of education through professional school, together with the earnings foregone (from age 14 forward), the total costs of a degree engineer's preparation was just over Rs. 19,000 (or U.S. $4,000 at the official exchange rate of that time). If the earnings foregone are excluded, according to Gounden's indications, the specifically educational costs come down to Rs. 10,200 (U.S. $2,150). If attention is focused on the professional education alone, (six years of "professional college" beyond the "matriculate" or high school level), total cost was just under Rs. 16,000 inclusive of earnings foregone; and was just over Rs. 9,000 for the specifically educational costs alone. These schooling costs are approximately confirmed by Blaug, Layard and Woodhall, using slightly different calculation methods.

To estimate the aggregate value of PTK emigration from India during the past decade, on our chosen basis of professional education only, without any earnings foregone, we first adjust the engineering educational costs—professional schooling only—to represent all professionals. To allow for more highly educated types (M.D.'s, Ph.D.'s) partly offset by less educated types (B.A.'s, B.Sc.'s, Engineering Diplomates), we raise the engineers' cost of Rs. 9,000 by an additional one-sixth (to represent one more year of schooling on the average), to Rs. 10,500 in 1960. Next we step up this figure by 20 per cent to 1965 cost levels (i.e., to Rs. 12,600); and by 50 per cent to 1969 cost levels (i.e., to Rs. 15,750); while 1971 was at 10 per cent above 1969 (i.e., at Rs. 17,300). These cost figures are then multiplied by the net PTK emigration numbers previously estimated for each of these dates, yielding the following aggregate values for each year. in then current prices:

           1965   Rs. 27.8 million
           1969   Rs. 31.6 million
           1971   Rs. 57.6 million

To go beyond these simple money amounts to their relative magnitudes, we compare them with India's figures in each year for total GDP, for total educational outlays (at all levels, but by public authorities only, in the absence of reliable figures for the private sector), and for net official foreign aid (total "official development assistance" from all foreign countries, less interest and amortization on old loans). These figures, so far as available at this time, are as follows, in millions of current rupees:

	GDP	Public educational outlays	Net official aid
1965	240,900	5,800	7,400
1969	368,200	9,200	8,250

For the year 1969, the aggregate cost of the net PTK emigration, as defined just above to amount to 31.6 million rupees, comes to less than .01 of 1 per cent of India's GDP, and to .35 of 1 per cent of that country's public outlays on education, and to .4 of 1 per cent of the net official aid received in that year. Looking at the trend during the 1960's, we find that in 1965 the first two percentages were slightly larger than in 1969, while the percentage of foreign aid was smaller than in 1969. For 1971, according to our rough estimates, the first two percentages were again slightly larger than in 1969, while the percentage of foreign aid (which has declined somewhat below the 1969 level) has risen to about .8 of 1 per cent.

As the cost of emigration used here is a narrowed figure obtained by a number of exclusions from the gross figures, it may be useful to indicate the outside magnitudes when all the exclusions are put back. For 1969, this means .07 of 1 per cent of GDP, 2.5 per cent of educational outlays, and 2.8 per cent of net aid. For 1971, the first two percentages should be raised by about half, while the aid percentage rises to about 5 per cent.

No doubt, educational costs in India are exceptionally low (converting rupee values into U.S. $ at the then prevailing exchange rate of 4.76 per $). For all levels of education plus estimated foregone earnings, the preparation of a degree engineer in India cost $4,000 as of 1960. This was below one-seventh of the comparable U.S. cost.[31]

If foregone earnings are excluded from the above calculation, the eduational inputs alone come to $2,150 and $13,430 for the two countries: a ratio of about one-sixth. In turn, if we focus only on the professional levels of education, and again exclude foregone earnings, the respective costs come to $1,900 and $5,800: a ratio of about one-third.

These cost-ratios, ranging between one-seventh and one-third, suggest that India has a large "absolute advantage" over the United States in the production of skilled personnel; probably the advantage would be somewhat reduced, but would remain quite large, in comparisons of India with various European countries. India may have an actual *comparative* advantage in education, as the above ratios to U.S. costs are probably far lower than those prevailing for most other services or commodities produced in the two countries. If the emigration of skilled personnel can be put on some acceptable exchange basis, or *quid pro quo,* India should specialize in the production of such personnel and export them. Instead of lamenting the outflow of most categories of skilled persons, Indian agencies—schools and universities, professional associations, manpower-planning bureaus—should consider the promotion of such exports on suitable terms. In some circles in New Delhi reached during a recent visit, interest was expressed in such a program.

IV. *Professional Emigration from Other Developing Nations*

The foregoing case of India is not unique. On the contrary, it is typical of a large class of developing countries.[32] These are nations where economic progress has been sufficiently strong to both encourage and support a great expansion of higher education; but the latter in turn outruns the needs of the economy and swamps its capacity to absorb additional professional personnel—even while the economy is growing at quite respectable rates, sometimes at quite high rates on a worldwide scale of economic performance.

An extreme case is the Philippines, whose annual gross numbers of emigrating PTK—around 9,000 a year to the United States alone, in recent years—has actually equalled or exceeded the outflow from vastly larger India.[33]

Other countries believed to be in a similar situation of surplus supplies of professionals, and substantial numbers of professional emigrants, include South Korea, Taiwan, Iran, Lebanon, Colombia, Guyana, and Barbados. Several other countries, such as Argentina, Haiti, and the U.A.R. were apparently in this class until recently, when revival of economic growth or other factors tended to reduce the emigration. Conversely, Thailand exemplifies a country which has only recently begun to show large numbers of PTK emigrants, in a trend now rising rapidly; and the reasons may be traced in large part to the expansion of higher education relative to the growth and absorptive capacity of the economy. Here we revert to the monitory tale, set forth at the beginning of this paper, of the new medical school that was built in the 1960's in Chiengmai in northern Thailand, in the hope of keeping a large proportion of the graduates in that region to serve provincial needs; and the shock of finding that most of the first graduating class chartered an airplane and flew off like a migratory flock to jobs in the United States.

For all the prevalence of the foregoing type, there are a number of developing countries of quite different types, where professionals are not in surplus supply. One of these types is exemplified by Venezuela, Brazil, Malaysia, Hongkong (if we exclude persons merely in transit through that entrepôt), and Japan (when it was still classified as a "developing country"). These are nations where economic progress is so strong that the growing supplies of professionals are usually absorbed into growing employment. An approximate balance is observed here at a high level, with little net emigration of professionals (Venezuela has a net *inflow*). To be sure in future such a country might develop a surplus of professionals whenever higher education accelerates and/or economic growth slows down. According to some recent indications, this phenomenon might well emerge in Japan during the next 5–10 years.

A quite different type is exemplified by Burma, Honduras, Indonesia, and some African nations until recently: countries where the economy has been so weak and sluggish that higher education is neither encouraged nor supported very much. Here the supply of professionals grows slowly, as does the demand for them. An approximate balance is observed at a low level. There is little net emigration of professionals, causing little loss to the economy, and in some instances some net gain from emigration.

By 1967, however, the rapid increase of Africans studying in universities at home or abroad began to stimulate emigration. This, in the face of moderate economic growth, might not have been troublesome, were it not for the political/cultural demand for "Africanization" of personnel.

V. *Some Policy Implications as to Professional Migration*

Our investigation has been intended to provide a conceptual analysis and a factual basis for understanding the brain drain in its several forms and directions, and thus illuminating the policy alternatives. Perhaps our most basic finding is the relatively small gains to the advanced nations receiving professional inflow, and the relatively small losses to the developing countries which as a group are experiencing net outflow. Next is our finding of three very different sub-groups of these developing countries: (1) countries showing large net emigration in terms of flow and stock ratios; this emigration flows from surplus supplies of professional and technical personnel, and therefore presents no acute problem, and perhaps presents an opportunity for beneficial exports; (2) countries showing small net emigration ratios (occasionally net immigration); these present no current problem, and little opportunity, as regards emigration—except perhaps the loss of some "key" personnel; (3) countries showing substantial net emigration in the face of overall shortages of professional and technical personnel, as shown by persistent real vacancies and low unemployment of professionals, and sometimes by their rising salaries.

Only the third and smallest sub-group of developing countries shows serious economic losses that demand vigorous policies and programs, of the kind usually proposed indiscriminately for all the developing countries. For this sub-group, several different types of programs may be distinguished: (a) to restrict emigration —whether by passport control, by exit fees, or by requirement of national service; (b) to induce remaining in the home country —whether by salary and fringe benefit increases, by expansion of research opportunities, by awards of prestige, or the like; (c) to demand compensation for the emigrants—whether by assessment on the individual emigrant at exit or when abroad (or on his family remaining in the home country), or by international agreements for government-to-government reimbursement from the receiving country to the country of origin.

Insofar as the losses suffered by these countries from emigration rest on the prevalence of a market economy and the free movement of persons, a simple reaction is to turn to programs of type *(a)*, which depart from the market and from mobility. These are generally viewed, however, as a distortion of efficient allocation of resources, and as an invasion of human freedom, specifically counter to the United Nations' Declaration of the Rights of Man. A notable exception seems to be public approval of compulsory national service by graduates in certain fields, especially in medical care; such a requirement was recently adopted in India and in Thailand, namely that new graduates of state-supported medical schools must serve for several years in underprivileged areas designated by public authorities and at civil-service rates of pay.

The orthodox market solution is to allow or encourage salaries to rise—for all scarce personnel. A more positive governmental line would in addition provide fringe benefits and other opporunities and amenities. But all these costs may well exceed the losses due to a certain percentage rate of emigration, and also exceed the expenses incurred by expanding education at home or abroad—or recruiting foreign professionals—in order to offset free emigration. These alternatives suggest that if the manpower authorities cannot afford to join the market, they had better prepare to beat it! In still larger terms, the planners must decide where the real national priorities lie—as regards favoring indigenous professionals, expanding educational systems, and promoting income equality as well as economic development—and stop trying to "put everything first."

The third avenue for dealing with real losses due to emigration is also a modification of the market, since the export of people is not ordinarily reimbursed like the export of goods or contractual services. The simplest form of this, namely requiring emigrants at the time of departure to repay to the state the costs of their education (or the estimated value of their output to be foregone), was instituted in the Soviet Union in 1972, but was widely denounced in principle as well as in its disproportionate impact on particular ethnic groups. A more acceptable device would be a fee to be delivered to the country of origin, paid either by the emigrant out of his subsequent earnings abroad over a period of years, or paid by the receiving country out of the national benefit obtained or expected from such emigrant. A particular instrument for this purpose, geared to the magnitude of such earnings and national benefit, would be a specific income surtax at appropriate rates, as suggested by Bhagwati and Dellalfar of M.I.T. in a recent article.[34]

As to the proper size of the payments: if we draw upon international trade theory here, the equilibrium price would fall between the actual (weighted average) cost of producing a professional in his country of origin and the opportunity cost of producing an equivalent in the receiving nation. On the other hand, if we draw upon human-capital theory, the compensation should be measured by the average migrant's productivity (whether current or capitalized), falling between his foregone contribution to output or welfare in his home country, and his actual or potential contribution in the receiving country.

Finally, all compensation should be based on net rather than gross emigration; and therefore must take account of student conversions, return flows, diversion into other occupations, remittances by expatriates and other adjustments which have been discussed in this paper and are still in need of much basic research.

As always in social and international issues, better data will resolve some debates, while rigorous analysis will untie some semantic knots, and will demonstrate the real constraints on wishful behavior ("you can't put everything first"); but the more recalcitrant problems lie elsewhere, in divergent values and conflicting interest-groups of people.

NOTES

1. Th. D. Dublin, "Migration of Physicians to U.S.," *New England Journal of Medicine*, Apr. 20, 1972, p. 6.

2. See: H. G. Johnson papers in W. Adams (ed.), *The Brain Drain* (Macmillan, 1968), and in G. Ranis (ed.), *The Gap between Rich and Poor Nations* (Macmillan, 1971); Grubel and Scott papers in *Amer. Ec. Rev.* , May 1966, and in *Jour. Pol. Econ.*, August, 1966; H. Myint paper in Adams volume, *cit. sup.;* E. J. Mishan paper in Inst. of Econ. Aff., *Economic Issues in Immigration* (1970). The neo-classical assumptions in this literature are criticized in a forthcoming "theoretical analysis" by J. Bhagwati and K. Hamada; but they actually use neo-classical mechanisms in trying to show losses from the brain drain.

3. See G. B. Baldwin, "Brain Drain or Overflow?," *Foreign Affairs*, Jan. 1970.

4. See particularly: S. Watanabe, "The Brain Drain from Developing to Developed Countries," *Int'l. Lab. Rev.*, April 1969; E. P. Reubens, *Migration and Development in the West Indies* (Univ. of the West Indies, 1962); OECD, *The International Movement of Scientists and Engineers* (Paris, 3 March 1970); Education and World Affairs, *The International Migration of High-Level Manpower* (Praeger, 1970); U.N., ECOSOC, *Outflow of Trained Personnel from Developing to Developed Countries* (E/4820, June 1970); N.S.F., *Scientists, Engineers and Physicians from Abroad: Trends through 1970* (Washington, 1972, N.S.F. 72-312); and N.S.F., *Immigrant Scientists and Engineers in the U.S.* (Washington, 1973, N.S.F. 73-302); also a forthcoming study by UNITAR on foreign students.

5. Derived from G. Hanoch in *Jour. Human Resources*, Summer 1967, Table 2.

6. See data on graduate studies in N.S.F. 73-302, Table B-8; also J. R. Niland, *The Asian Engineering Brain Drain* (Heath, 1970), pp. 35–36.

7. Based on O. Gish, *Doctor Migration and World Health* (Bell, 1971), Ch. III.

8. Educational costs estimated at £6,000 for B.Sc. in science and engineering, and £16,000 for Ph.D. in physics, according to Working Group on Migration, *The Brain Drain* (Cmnd. 3417, Oct. 1967), Chap. IV.

9. Percentages derived from data in OECD, *Int'l Movement, cit. sup.,* Tables 8 and 9. Same order of magnitude in Atkinson, Barnes and Richardson, *Canada's Highly Qualified Manpower Resources* (1970, Dept. Mnpr. and Immig., Canada).

10. Derived from U.S. I.N.S., *Annual Reports*, Tables 6C and 8, also *Annual Indicators of Immigration . . . in Professional and Related Occupations*, 1967–1970, charts 10 and 24; N.S.F. 72-312, *cit. sup.*, p. 6.

11. Return rate estimated at 25% of the gross inflows of Latin American professionals into U.S. during 1961–65 (Charles V. Kidd, statement published in *The Brain Drain into the U.S.: A Staff Study*, 90th Congress, H. of Rep., Washington, 1967, p. 105). Higher return rates for Asian immigrant professionals are suggested by data

for India (Institute of Applied Manpower Research, *The Brain Drain Study,* New Delhi, 1970, pp. 45–47) and by British accumulations between the two censuses of 1961 and 1966. More definitive figures for U.S. migration must wait for the publication of 1970 U.S. census reports.

12. Percentage for 1966 derived from OECD, *cit. sup.,* Tables 8 and 9. Percentage for 1970 derived from N.S.F., 72-312, *cit. sup.,* p. 18.

13. Derived from data in R. Stevens and J. Vermeulen, *Foreign Trained Physicians and American Medicine* (H.E.W., 1972), p. 104.

14. Derived from N.S.F. 72-312, p. 1, adjusted for LDC-origins.

15. Derived from Dublin, *cit. sup.,* p. 2.

16. *Mo. Labor Review,* Oct. 1972, p. 9.

17. U.S. Dept of Labor, *Manpower Report of the President,* March 1973, p. 19.

18. Stevens and Vermeulen, pp. 16–17.

19. Derived from Stevens and Vermeulen, Tables D4 and D7.

20. Direct educational cost data, and estimated net income foregone, from A. M. Carter paper in Chamberlain (ed.), *Contemporary Economic Issues* (Irwin, 1969), pp. 148–50; also Grubel and Scott, *J.P.E.,* Aug. 1966, Table 1; also Vredeveld paper in the present volume; also Wing and Blumberg paper in *Jour. Human Resources,* Winter 1971. Unit costs have been combined by applying estimated weights for the several immigrating categories and their respective educational levels.

21. Gross inflow of 11,000 per year, reduced for student conversions and return flows during 1962–66.

22. Based on data from chief receiving countries (sources as cited in Table 2) supplemented by N.S.F. reports, also Watanabe, *cit. sup.,* Table I.

23. Derived from I.N.S., *Annual Indicator, 1969,* charts 3 and 24.

24. See I.A.M.R., *cit. sup.,* Table 18; Gish, p. 41; Blaug, Layard and Woodhall, *The Causes of Graduate Unemployment in India* (Penguin, 1969), p. 155; N.S.F. 73–302, App. Table B-23.

25. See Footnote 11.

26. C.S.I.R., *Technical Manpower* (New Delhi), April 1972.

27. I.L.O., *Yearbook of Labor Statistics,* annual, Table 2B. Also OECD, *Occupational and Educational Structures . . . and Economic Development* (Paris, 1970), Graph II-1, p. 54.

28. See particularly I.A.M.R., *Employmnet Outlook for Engineers, 1969–79* (New Delhi, 1969).

29. *Op. cit.,* p. 250.

30. A. M. Nalla Gounden, "Investment in Education in India," *Jour. Human Resources,* Summer 1967; Blaug, Layard and Woodhall, *cit. sup.,* Tables 8.10 and 8.12.

31. $28,995 as calculated by Grubel and Scott, *J.P.E.,* Aug. 1966, p. 369.

32. Cf. the region-by-region examination in Baldwin, *cit. sup., For. Aff.,* Jan. 1970, pp. 364–67.

33. For information on Philippine education for emigration purposes, see M. L. Gupta, "Outflow of High-Level Manpower from the Philippines," *Int'l. Lab. Rev.,* Feb. 1973, especially pp. 181–84.

34. J. Bhagwati and W. Dellalfar, "The Brain Drain and Income Taxation," *World Development,* Feb. 1973.

Comments on "*The New Brain Drain from Developing Countries:*
International Costs and Benefits, 1960-1972"

James M. Arrowsmith*

I want to begin by discussing the appropriate measure of the cost
of an out-migrating professional to his mother country and the benefit of this in-migrating professional to the advanced country into
which he immigrates. Professor Reubens raises two types of question about the measurement of this respective cost and benefit. Included in the first is whether the cost of the out-migrant should be
measured by the cost of his production or preparation, or by the
present value of his lifetime product. Surely, in general, the relevant measure is the latter, what Professor Reubens calls the "opportunity cost" of the migrant. Whatever the professional out-migrant
cost to produce, bygones are bygones and the cost of his out-
migration is his foregone output; if that be zero, then his out-
migration costs nothing. The only exception to this would be where
the society from which the professional migrated insisted on replac-
ing every out-migrant by training another person to take his place.
In that case, the cost of out-migration would be the cost of training
the professional.[1] Similarly in general the benefit of an immigrant
professional to the recipient country is to be measured by the present value of his lifetime contribution to production, rather than by
the what it would have cost to train an equivalent, native-born professional in the recipient country. Again there is an exception to
this if the recipient country would have followed a replacement policy, training a native professional if the foreign professional had
not immigrated. In this case the benefit to the recipient country is
the saved cost of training a native professional, where this cost
being saved includes the present value of the lifetime output of the

*The author is now at the Department of Justice. He was an Assistant Professor of
    Economics at the City College of the City University of New York when he deli-
    vered these comments.

native in the occupation he would have followed if he had not been trained as a professional. It does seem plausible to argue that such a replacement policy does sometimes operate in recipient countries, and therefore I would tend to argue that the cost of out-migration to mother countries is best measured by the foregone earnings, although the benefit of immigration to recipient countries may sometimes be measured by the "avoided costs of educating another native to professional qualifications."

The second type of question raised refers to the appropriate measure of a professional immigrant's contribution to total product in the event that it is considered appropriate to use this as a measure of the benefit of his immigration. Professor Reubens argues that this contribution to total product should be measured only by the excess of the immigrant professional's lifetime earnings over what a non-professional native earns in his lifetime. I think that his position is erroneous, since it is not only the professional part of the immigrant that adds to output—his brawn power immigrates as much as does his brain power. Thus if one uses lifetime earnings as a measure of benefit, the whole lifetime earnings is the appropriate measure. Even this, however, tends to understate the immigrant's contribution to total output since all except the last immigrant professional contribute more to total output than they receive in earnings. The relevance of my remarks, of course, is to the evaluation of the data on the value of the inflow of migrants to Britain, Canada, and the United States. If some estimate of the present value of the lifetime earnings of professionals immigrating to these countries from the less developed countries were computed, it is likely that it would be larger than the estimates of the saved costs of training natives which Professor Reubens uses as a basis for his estimate of the benefits of professional immigration. To the extent, then, that these countries did not follow a replacement policy, Professor Reubens' estimates understate the importance of the reverse foreign aid provided by the brain drain.

On the other hand, to the extent that these countries did follow a replacement policy, their reliance on any professional immigration, from less developed countries or anywhere else, poses a serious question of equity as distinct from the maximization of national income. Under such circumstances, immigration of n professionals means that n natives are not trained to professional levels and presumably remain in lower-paid, less desirable occupations. In the absence of immigration, the ratio of professional to other workers would be higher and presumably the inequality of incomes lower. In addition, it is likely that a disproportional number of native professionals who would be trained in the absence of professional immigration—and who are not trained *because* of this immigration—would come from those groups who have tended to be hampered in obtaining professional training by barriers of social and economic class, race, sex, or age. In short, immigration, on the replacement theory, has buttressed inequality.

If we now turn to consider the effects of professional outmigration on the mother countries, Professor Reubens, in his study of the Indian case, has provided an important illustration of the point that for some kinds of professional labor from some less developed countries out-migration imposes no loss of national production since this labor is surplus. Unless these countries follow a replacement policy this professional immigration is costless. Since there is no evidence that India does follow a replacement policy I would strongly disagree with Professor Reubens' estimate that the net outflow of professionals from India represented a loss to that country of $15.3 million. The loss was zero. Indeed if one wishes to consider the saving in consumption in India and any immigrant remittances, the loss was negative!

At this point let me turn to consider the suggestion that India should specialize in the production of professional personnel and export them to countries that would be willing to pay for their service since in that way they could acquire professionals more cheaply than by producing them domestically. In such a case, both India and the recipient countries would be operating on the basis of a replacement policy, and the cost of production of a professional in India and in the recipient countries would, of course, be the relevant measure of cost and benefit from the migration. In such a case, if we make the simplifying assumption that in both groups of countries government bears all costs of professional training, the payments by recipient countries to India would be both equitable compensation and the basis for an international specialization in the production of human capital. However, since it is not apparent that recipient countries do always operate on a replacement basis, it is not obvious that this suggestion has direct relevance to the present professional out-migration from India to the United States and other developed countries. Since, as I have noted above, the re-placement policy itself may have serious weaknesses when consider-ations of equity are taken into account, the desirability of this kind of trade is questionable even where it is relevant.

To return to the mainstream of Professor Reubens' paper, I would certainly agree with his strong emphasis on the different impact that professional out-migration has on different less de-veloped countries' economics, with some enjoying a a negative loss from at least some kinds of professional outmigration while others suffer a positive loss from most or all professional out-migration, many African nations especially falling into the latter category. In short, I feel it not unfair to characterize his position as being that for some less developed countries all or most professional out-migration and for other less developed countries some professional out-migration implies economic losses. The immigration of these professionals into developed countries produces aggregate economic gains for those countries. It seems reasonable to assume that the flow of professional migration is from countries of lower to countries of higher social marginal productivity of professional labor, so that in terms of output the developed countries' gains ex-ceed the less developed countries' losses and world output is in-creased as a result of this migration. Implicit in Professor Reubens' whole paper, however, are two propositions; The first is that the less developed countries are concerned with their loss and are not comforted by the knowledge that it is less than developed country increases in production. The second is that even from a world point of view the increase in world product associated with profes-sional migration may be associated not with an increase but with a decrease in world welfare if the utility of the income lost by de-veloping countries exceeds the utility of the income gained by the developed countries. Additionally, since the developed countries apparently gain utility from giving aid to less developed countries, presumably they lose utility when they receive aid from less developed countries.

I am in fundamental agreement with this view that the brain drain has economic effects which are undesirable. Although the magnitude of the drain and of the economic effects should not be exaggerated, policy measures should be undertaken to prevent those effects occurring. Where I might perhaps disagree with Professor Reubens is on the policy measures which I should recommend.

Broadly speaking, there are two types of policy measures which are relevant. The first is measures to prevent the migration of professional workers from less developed countries to developed countries. The second is arrangements for the beneficiary recipient countries to compensate the losing countries from which the professionals migrate. Under the first category of measures fall policies of restriction of emigration by the less developed countries or restriction of immigration by the developed recipient countries. Since, accurately, emigration restriction is considered more restrictive of civil liberties than immigration restriction (in a world of more than two countries[2] the prevention of the brain drain would require the prohibition of the immigration of all those professionals from less developed countries where out-migration imposed an economic loss upon their countries of origin. This type of policy would be perfectly feasible and would require no increase in the degree of bureaucratic input into the control of immigration in the United States.

The present immigration legislation requires prospective immigrants to supply large amounts of detailed occupational and other information which is currently used as tha basis for determining admissibility. It would be a simple matter for the governments of those developing countries wishing to stop the migration of scarce professionals to the developed countries to supply the U.S. and other governments with a list of those professions whose members they wished excluded from developed countries. It cannot accurately be claimed that this kind of immigration policy would be any more unfair than the present immigration legislation of the developed countries. In the case of the United States, for example, the liberalization of immigration law in 1965 merely replaced racial discrimination with discrimination in favor of alien relatives of U.S. citizens and well educated aliens. It cannot surely be argued that it is more ethical to discriminate against Irish laborers and in favor of Indian doctors than against Indian doctors and in favor of Irish laborers.

If this trend of immigration policy in the developed countries is considered unacceptable, it would seem desirable for the recipient countries to provide additional foreign aid to compensate the countries losing professional workers. Indeed it might be desirable to make these aid payments retroactive to cover the brains that have drained since 1945. Of course, the basis for the aid would be the value of the lost output in the migrants' countries of origin, *not* their cost of training.

With my own suggestions to provide background, let me challenge Professor Reubens' conclusion that one solution to the brain drain is to raise salaries and multiply jobs in the countries suffering the drain. While I would agree where professionals' wages are deliberately kept below professionals' marginal productivity through governmental monopsony power, institutional reforms to raise wages to equal marginal productivity might check migration and are not undesirable in themselves. But even if professional wages are equal to marginal productivity, they will be lower in most occupations in most less developed countries because marginal productivity will be lower. Raising wages above marginal productivity levels would simply disemploy professionals and bring about similar effects to their emigration. It might be possible to raise incomes to developed country levels by supplementing marginal productivity wages with transfer payments financed by the rest of the population, but I find the equity implications of this rather disquieting.

NOTES

1. I assumed that this training cost exceeds his expected lifetime contribution to production.

2. Unless the countries restricting immigration collude in a cartel-like arrangement as Western countries did to restrict Jewish refugees in the period 1930–50.